The American Experiment

Perspectives on 200 Years

The American Experiment

☆☆☆☆☆☆☆☆☆☆☆☆☆☆☆☆☆☆☆☆☆☆☆☆☆☆☆☆☆☆☆☆☆☆☆☆☆

Perspectives on 200 Years

EDITED BY
Sam Bass Warner, Jr.

HOUGHTON MIFFLIN COMPANY
BOSTON 1976

Nov 15, 76

75 - 43762

ISBN: 0-395-24008-5 *cloth*
ISBN: 0-395-24007-7 *paper*

Printed in the United States of America

Listed april, 76.

V 10 9 8 7 6 5 4 3 2 1

The preservation of the sacred fire of liberty, and the destiny of the republican model of government, are justly considered as deeply, perhaps as finally staked, on the experiment entrusted to the hands of the American people.

GEORGE WASHINGTON
First Inaugural Address, 1789

Preface

I AM REMINDED every day of the American Revolution and the first 200 years of American life. My office overlooks Faneuil Hall, scene of many of the speeches and debates that helped to start the Revolution. For more than 200 years, while patriots and politicians held forth in the hall above, butchers and greengrocers plied their trades in the shops beneath. Faneuil Hall and its markets are a constant reminder that ideas are as essential to human nourishment as food.

From City Hall I also look out at the old granite warehouses that made Boston a great center of nineteenth-century trade and commerce. They stood empty and silent for years as new patterns of trade and technology made them obsolete. Now these buildings are coming to life again as apartments and shops for a modern city. They are handsome reminders to public officials and citizens that we must not lightly discard what past generations struggled to build.

To the right, looking out my office window, is a huge hole that will soon be filled by a new office building. In two or three years several thousand people will work there at the service jobs that are making Boston once more a center of American development.

An ugly expressway cuts through my picture of American history, where cars and trucks noisily belch pollution into the air. They are a dangerous reminder that we have let technology and "progress" get out of control.

These symbols surround the people of Boston every day. They give us a sense of place and continuity, whether we hark back to the *Mayflower*, the nineteenth-century steamers from Ireland and Italy, or are recent pilgrims ourselves. But these physical reminders, strong as they are, represent only a small part of what we are celebrating in the nation's Bicentennial.

The American Revolution was one of ideas as well as events. Any true commemoration must review the present state of those ideas. After the events of recent years it is important to ask whether those ideas have survived as well as the building in which they were first given tongue. Are the concepts of equality, procedural fairness, limited government, and inalienable rights still valid hallmarks for this country?

As a practicing politician I am aware of the gaps that exist between the ideals represented by the American revolution and the realities we face each day. I have not grown immune to the human suffering caused by hatred, injustice, and inequality. In fact, I think the pain is greater now.

Boston has severe racial problems. Simply put, blacks and whites have not yet learned to live together in peace and mutual respect. The sense of fairness and equality that helped start the American Revolution does not yet dominate our dealings with people of another color. The problem is so severe it threatens all the progress we have made in other fields. Our dramatic legal progress in human rights turns to myth when the police are forced to keep crowds of black and white children from beating each other. It is an ugly and a frightening sight.

Despite the present national recession, Boston is in the midst of an economic boom fueled by the change to a service-based economy. Yet 20 percent of our residents are on one form of welfare or another, and about 25 percent are either unemployed or involuntarily underemployed. The sense of equity and justice for all which brought wealthy merchants and poor laborers together in the Revolution seems weak and ailing in modern Boston. The experts describe it as a "mismatch" between skills and jobs. That is too cold a term. Beneath the surface of our economic revival is a sea of human tragedy and waste. That cannot be the picture the founders meant us to be looking at on our two-hundredth birthday.

Because so much remains to be done, I believe that our Bicentennial celebration must include a serious discussion of the problems we face in this city and society, and the relevance of the revolutionary ideas which flourished here 200 years ago. This book, I hope, will be a significant contribution to the debate.

Frankly, my motivation for holding these "Forums" was partly selfish. I wanted an opportunity to place some of the problems I face every day in an historical context that might provide guidance and perspective. But I also felt an obligation to Sam Adams. His statue also can be seen from my window. He stands slightly askew, arms folded and toe tapping impatiently. I am sure he wants to hear how we are doing. We owe it to him — and to ourselves.

KEVIN H. WHITE
Mayor of Boston

Contents

About This Book

THIS IS an unusual book. It has been written by hundreds of Americans. It reprints a group of addresses delivered in the spring of 1975 and reports on the reactions to them of audiences in downtown Boston, of political, business, and educational leaders, and of radio audiences across the country. It is not offered as an authoritative view of the United States of America on the occasion of its anniversary. Rather, it is a reflection of the way thoughtful Americans felt about their nation, their traditions, and their future, on that occasion.

Whether you, reader, are on a Bicentennial visit and have picked up this book for an interval of reading, or whether you are sitting at home or in a library, you are participating in the Bicentennial observance. You are joining thousands of your fellow citizens in making a serious assessment of the nation, its hopes, and its troubles.

The initial effort which began this process was a continuation of an old American civic tradition — the joint venture of the merchant and the public official. Many of the libraries, art museums, philanthropies, and civic ornaments of our cities have their origins in such unions. In this one, Abram T. Collier, Chairman, New England Mutual Life Insurance Company, wanted the Bicentennial observances in Boston to include, as well as exhibits, parades, and the reenactment of battles, some thoughtful public consideration of the state of the nation. The suggestion was of immediate interest to Boston's Mayor Kevin H. White, and from it evolved "The Bicentennial Forums: Boston Examines the American Experiment," jointly sponsored by New England Life, the Parkman Center for Urban Affairs — the city's research and thinking center — and Boston 200, the city's Bicentennial agency. Each of the five "Forums" in the series consisted of three major events: an address by a distinguished scholar or political leader, followed by questions from the diverse audience of Boston residents, a discussion at the Parkman Center by the speaker and a score of invited civic and educational leaders, and a broadcast of the address over National Public Radio followed by questions phoned in from listeners across the nation, answered and discussed by a panel of experts in Boston, Washington, D.C., and sometimes other cities.

No requirements were laid down for the speakers beyond the request that they seriously consider the state of the nation on the occasion of its Bicentennial. The speakers took up very different themes: the corporate transformation of American society, the maintenance of civil liberties in the face of the need for big government, the collapse of domestic and foreign policy as a consequence of a new style of image-making governance, the increase in the accountability of the office of the President, and the dangers of no-action government and the possibilities of decentralized management of public programs.

The five addresses and the discussions which followed moved out from these themes to a consideration of most current issues in American public life: foreign policy, military expenditures, race relations, campaign financing, corporate governance and control, labor unions, women's liberation,

xiv

public education, political leadership, bureaucracy, the media, national economic and ecological planning, wages and employment, health care, taxation, and urban finance. The participants showed genuine concern for the nation and its well-being, and while some were confident that the country is weathering its trials, others feared that its proper goals were far from being realized.

There is thus immense variety of opinion in the text that follows, and a great deal of sincere feeling. No reader will agree with everything that is said, yet through all its variety in feeling and belief, the book reveals a deep cohesiveness in most American opinion. Two schools of thought are not here represented, though both have many adherents in the land: the socialist left and the political right. Rather, the speakers and their several audiences speak within the broad framework of current interpretations of the Constitution of 1787 as those interpretations today define individual liberty, private property, and political institutions.

It is our hope that the book will assist the reader in making his own assessment of the nation at the time of its Bicentennial. To stimulate this process let us look back at the state of the nation on the date of its Centennial a hundred years ago.

In 1876 the nation was in the midst of a deep, five-year depression. John D. Rockefeller, like others in his generation of new millionaires, was consolidating his empire by legal and illegal means. The Molly Maguires were murdering their opponents in a bitter coal strike in Pennsylvania. And a Yale professor published a book saying that the workers of America did not receive the highest wages possible and would not fare well until they owned the mines and factories of the nation. Waves of European immigrants poured into the country and its cities. The North was tiring in its efforts to secure the civil rights of blacks in the former Confederate states, although South Carolina, Florida, and Louisiana were still occupied by federal troops. The war for the extermination of the American Indian continued unabated, and in June General Custer and his troops were routed at Little Bighorn, South Dakota.

The year was punctuated by periodic revelations of corruption in the administration of President Grant. His confidential secretary proved to be at the center of the Whisky Ring, a league of Internal Revenue agents, local politicians, and distillers who had combined to defraud the government of millions in tax revenues. The Secretary of War was proved to be guilty of graft in military contracts. He resigned hastily with the connivance of the President in order to escape impeachment and criminal prosecution. The November presidential election was so corruptly managed that Samuel J. Tilden, the Democratic candidate who received a majority of the popular vote, was counted out by fraudulent certification of ballots. Both Tilden and his opponent, later President Rutherford B. Hayes, were shown to be cheating on their federal income taxes, war levies then still in effect.

At Philadelphia the nation held its first World's Fair, a Centennial exhibition whose principal attractions were the new machines and products of the nation. Unaccountably to many males, the fair included a separate Women's Exhibition. Many of the sermons and orations delivered that year looked backward, not toward the future. Above all, speakers took pride in the survival of the new republic, especially after the terrible Civil War — its century of existence as a democratic experiment in a world composed of monarchies.

Here in Boston in 1976 we are continuing our celebration of the Bicentennial. The Forums, of which this book commemorates the first series, will go on. We will also revive the old custom of the Liberty Pole — a place where citizens can post their views on the political issues of the day. This time the pole will not be at the edge, but at the center of the town, where passers-by can use it and read what each day's comments offer. As a reader of this book we invite you to join us in this custom of informal political expression. You may mail your reactions to the issues raised in this book, your comments on the state of the nation, or your hopes for its future to: Liberty Pole, Boston 200, One Beacon Street, Boston, Massachusetts 02108.

SAM BASS WARNER, JR.

The American Experiment

Perspectives on 200 Years

1

On Celebrating
American Independence

Abram T. Collier

Late in the 1860s, a group of eminent Bostonians gathered to discuss the possibility of mounting an international exposition in 1875. Less than two decades before, in 1851, the first such exhibition had been held in the Crystal Palace in London. Another great exposition had been held in Paris four years later. What more appropriate kind of celebration could Boston have to commemorate the beginnings of independence in America?

After the members of the group had dined together for over a year, discussed sites, financing, and organization, they learned a dismaying fact: a similar group with similar objectives was meeting in Philadelphia. A delegation was dispatched from the Hub of the Universe to the City of Brotherly Love. The result might have been foreseen: Love conquered the Universe. The traveling Bostonians returned with the quite unremarkable recommendation that Boston should give way and concede to Philadelphia sole rights to the major celebration.

As matters turned out, Boston received recompence for this rare display of civic restraint in two respects: first, the most popular exhibit at the Centennial in Philadelphia was a device invented by a Boston resident, Alexander Graham Bell; second, members of the Boston group discovered they had so enjoyed dining together, they reconstituted themselves as The Beacon Society, with the result that they and their successors have been dining together ever since.

Early in the 1960s, a group of eminent Bostonians gathered to discuss the possibility of mounting an international exposition in Boston in 1975. They were confident that the Bostonian who occupied the White House would cooperate in petitioning the Bureau International des Expositions in Paris for authority under the existing international treaties to make Boston the site for a 1975 World's Fair. While John Kennedy did sign such a petition, his successor withdrew it and became so preoccupied with other matters that grand plans for the Bicentennial foundered nationally and no great exposition was mounted in Boston or in any other American city.

In any case, it is possible to argue that the days of the great fairs are over. Great fairs in Chicago and New York are better remembered for Sally Rand and Gypsy Rose Lee than for all the marvels of technology and commerce which were brought together. And quite possibly if large sums are to be spent by government and industry, they can better be spent on rebuilding our blemished cities than on midways and carnivals.

But birthdays are not to be ignored. There is something so fundamental in the birthday of an individual, or of a nation, that it may no more be ignored than the sun, the rain, or the stars. We may pretend indifference, we may brush off those who would declare a holiday, we may assert all celebrations to be childishness, but so long as America lives as a single nation, the days and years of its birth will be remembered. For any nation that loses touch with its beginnings may truly be said no longer to exist; it has become a different nation.

What are the functions of birthdays? Why should they be

celebrated by persons, or by governments? Let me offer several related answers.

Self-Esteem

One of the great social psychologists of our time, Erich Fromm, has expressed profound insights into the nature of love, especially an individual's power to love in relation to his power to work, to be independent, and to be truly free. Basic to his thought is the concept that no person can love another unless that person first loves himself. Many of us grew up with the idea that self-love was wrong, as indeed it is when carried to narcissistic extremes. What we so often fail to realize is that one must have a reasonable regard for one's self in order to love one's neighbors.

Consider the thoughts of a child on his birthday. The event carries enormous meaning. Feeling small in relation to the world about him, the child (like Pooh, the Bear of Very Small Brain) feels a pleasant surprise. "These people have baked a cake for me! They are bringing presents to me! They are singing for me! How can it be true?" Though the child may have felt a mother's and a father's love, here is evidence that he or she is well regarded in a wider circle. By these actions at a peculiarly *personal* event, the child acquires another layer of self-esteem, or to use the Oriental expression, the child "is given face."

As the child acquires pride, confidence, and self-esteem through the birthday celebration, so does the nation. While Independence Day has been accepted as the nation's birthday, other holidays celebrate other great events in our history. Columbus Day takes us back to the first Europeans on this continent, Thanksgiving to the first Pilgrims. We celebrate the birthdays of two Presidents who played key roles in our development. We devote two more days: Memorial (or Decoration) Day and Armistice (or Veterans) Day, to those individuals who gave their lives to the defense of the nation and its liberties.

This past summer Alexander Solzhenitsyn visited this country. Signing the guest book at Williamsburg, he wrote, "With great respect and admiration for the tradition here preserved . . . Woe to those nations that cut off those traditions by severing them with an ax." Whether Russia or any other nation can rewrite history is questionable. Russians as well as Americans need the self-esteem that comes from pride in their origins, their heroes, and their traditions.

Today "chauvinism" is one of our most pejorative terms, for it represents the excessive self-love that has led to at least two great wars in this century. And these nationalistic extremes have made many thoughtful persons question their allegiance to any national sovereignty, believing it is possible to think only as citizens of the world. This reaction to excessive nationalism seems to us unrealistic. We do not need to agree with all the attitudes of our families or our friends to feel love and loyalty for them. And as citizens we do not need to agree with all our nation's current policies to love it and to cherish our citizenship. But as Erich Fromm has suggested with respect to individual relationships, we cannot deal openly, effectively, or understandingly with other nations unless we can think well of our own.

Faith

If the Bicentennial is an essential exercise in building the nation's self-esteem and assisting in its relations with other nations, it may also be essential to the life of the nation in terms of its own internal health.

In our daily lives we give high priority to facts, to the things we know, to the accuracy of our knowledge. Even in matters of opinion, we have high confidence in reason, that free and open discussion and debate will produce solutions if worked at rationally by men of good will. What we often ignore is that the oil which lubricates our social machinery is not knowledge and reason, but faith.

To survive, a nation must have faith in its Constitution and its leaders, or at least most of them. It must have faith in its system of doing business, in its sense of what is right and wrong, fair or unfair. To have such faith is to transcend "facts." It is the kind of faith ultimately associated with belief in a divine being and man's relationship to that being. In no respect can these articles of faith be demonstrated by reason. As Ruth Benedict showed in *Patterns of Culture,* man can operate effective social systems with quite different types of faith. But the need for unquestioning acceptance of *some* articles of faith, which all or nearly all can accept, seems essential to social stability.

How we acquire our more profound beliefs is not entirely clear. Obviously they are inculcated in us at an early age, and they appear to grow out of habit and the rituals to which mystery and significance are attached. To these rituals we bring an attitude of reverence, and from them comes a deep respect for certain symbols. Rituals and symbols of secular institutions can be quite evidently as powerful as those of their religious counterparts.

The rituals of citizenship are many. The flag is early an object of care and veneration. Later, students are encouraged to engage in self-government, to listen to and absorb the holiday proclamations of Presidents and governors. We give formal assent to the Constitution when we register to vote. We march in holiday parades and lay wreaths on the graves of heroes.

Many of us who grew up when the Fourth of July was celebrated with firecrackers and two-inch salutes, with torpedoes and carbide cannons, feel that something went out of that holiday when these noisemakers were banned. Reason said they were dangerous, but a holiday is a time for brave and even dangerous deeds, and in the ritual of the "old Fourth" we relived in symbolic form the dangers our ancestors braved and the wars they fought in.

Identity

Arnold Toynbee speaks of the self-centeredness of historians. "The historian," he said, "is a prisoner of his own time and place; . . . his only standing ground for viewing the upper reaches of the river of history is the constantly moving locus of the masthead of the little boat in which the observer himself is traveling all the time down the lower reaches of the same ever-rolling stream." Thus, he says, each generation imposes its own perspective on each epoch of history.

While historians value objectivity and make bona fide attempts to overcome their self-centeredness, most people are participants in history rather than observers. They are actors, caught in one particular moment of history, enmeshed in a web of loyalties and obligations. They cannot be objective, for they must act, and act in relation to others. They must behave as sons or daughters, as brothers or sisters, as fathers or mothers. To earn a livelihood they join institutions, professions, or trades. They live in a particular city or town and become citizens of a particular state or nation.

Wherever they go, whatever they do, their relationships determine the roles they play. While these roles deny them the objectivity of the historian, they do develop their sense of individuality and separate identity.

Few dilemmas are more difficult than the problems created by amnesty for those who evaded the draft during the Vietnam war by moving abroad. Like perhaps a majority of the nation, they regarded the war as fighting in the wrong place, at the wrong time, and for the wrong reasons. Yet the price of moving out of their country was the relinquishing, temporarily or permanently, of a critical element of their identity. The debate over the conditions of their return shows the intensity of their feelings and the feelings of all those whose citizenship helps to define their being.

The great celebrant of the American identity was, of course, Walt Whitman. While there was much he questioned and despaired of in the land, he celebrated himself as an American when he heard America singing and as he sang of himself. He did not ask for good fortune, for he believed that he himself was good fortune. Strong and content, he traveled America's open road. Under the splendid silent sun, under the immense and silent moon, he believed the United States themselves were the greatest of poems.

To be a citizen is to share to some extent Whitman's joy and identity as an American. We may not be objective observers of our history, but we are active, concerned participants in it.

Purpose

The last, and for many, the only reason we celebrate our beginnings is to determine not what we *have* done but what we *ought* to do. We may reasonably take pride in our past, yet we must recognize that there has been a vast distance between what we have done and what we ought to have done. A celebration gives us a chance to take stock, to consider what courses of action can bring us closer to the enduring American Dream.

Without question, America's self-confidence has been deeply shaken by recent events:

> we discovered that we could not, by military or other means, bring about peace in Southeast Asia
> we discovered that our institutions could not cope with worldwide inflation and shrinking international resources
> we discovered that we could not even control the value of our own money
> we discovered that we could not easily or quickly integrate minorities into the mainstream of American life
> we discovered that we could elect to high office a man who could not admit his misdeeds and compounded them by lying to the people

And so it is no wonder that many have begun to question our human and political institutions, and to develop a collective sense of imminent frustration and defeat. Do we need more intervention by government in social and economic affairs, or less? If intervention, what kind? What national goals can we agree on? Can they be achieved? What changes, if any, do we need in the fundamental law of the land, the Constitution?

"It is not what man *does* which exalts him," wrote Robert Browning, "but what man would do!" We live not so much by assessing where we are as by assessing where we are going. At the moment, many people do not feel exalted; rather, they feel that *things* are in the saddle. They would be happier if they could sense some worthier purpose.

Yet it may not be amiss to observe that in spite of our evident troubles:

the United States is still governed by a basic law that has been operative since 1787

we have successfully survived one war that threatened to tear the nation in two, and two wars that threatened to overwhelm the rest of the world

we have so far survived a social and technological revolution that, in less than a century, has transferred 90 percent of our population from the farms to the cities

for the first time in history we have created a society which is not only literate but lives in a degree of affluence not dreamed of a century ago

Far from being diminished by our recent turbulence, we should therefore feel a sense of exaltation in the knowledge that our political structure can survive such stresses and strains. As a steadily pioneering nation, optimism becomes us.

The dominant rhetoric of our time, Ben Wattenberg has suggested, should not be of failure, guilt, and crisis, but of progress, growth, and success. Wattenberg may go too far — for America does not live alone by bread, by knowledge, by experience, or even by the most sophisticated forms of culture. America, like any nation, lives — in the last analysis — on a sense of purpose shared by all its citizens. The transcendent test today — in science, art, religion, and society — is whether we can once again aspire to great ideals as individuals and as a nation.

The opening of China in recent years has exposed a paradox. A nation that for several centuries had been weak and divided now appears under Communist leadership to have come together with a shared purpose, a dedication to self-sufficiency, a highly puritanical social life, and a complete denial of the existence of God.

The answer to this paradox must lie in Chinese tradition, which has never stressed the concept of an almighty being,

9

but has always celebrated human life and human relationships. Thus Marxian materialism may be of less importance in Chinese communism than the fact that the Chinese
people, like the Puritans and the nineteenth-century immigrants to these shores, are now working with a shared purpose. Perhaps they have a vision of what ought to be and
what can be, a vision of a society that can be better for their
children and their children's children than for themselves.

In sum, the celebration of American Independence may
have many objectives and many modes. The form of celebration in the Bicentennial Forums has been a fairly serious one,
bringing together a number of keen observers and analysts.
Each of them has expressed a "sense of the occasion" and a
sense of where, as a nation, we should be going. Each has
also expressed, I think, a degree of thankfulness for being an
American and the civility that goes with the commemoration
of great events.

2

The Two Revolutions

SAM BASS WARNER, JR.

The opening lecture of the Bicentennial Forums was given in Boston's historic Faneuil Hall on an exciting windswept February afternoon. The audience picked their way past heaps of earth and cobbles among workmen creating a new park and plaza at this old corner of downtown Boston. Up the steep stairs over the meat markets which still occupy the ground floor, they entered a gracious colonnaded hall with balconies on three sides, a space closer in feeling to a colonial meeting house than a modern lecture hall.

A graceful example of New England Georgian, Faneuil Hall was built in 1742. In the early years of the Republic it was enlarged by America's first name architect, Charles Bulfinch, and made almost three times its original size.

On a high platform, the speaker and the dignitaries who introduced him were framed by a gigantic painting of Webster replying to Hayne in the Senate in 1830: "Liberty and Union, Now and Forever." There are portraits and busts of Washington, John Adams, Lincoln, and of New England heroes of the Revolution and the Civil War. Known locally as "the Cradle of Liberty," the hall is a remarkable summary of Boston civic tradition as it was up to a hundred years ago.

Introducing the series and the speaker were Abram T. Collier, Chairman of New England Life, and Mayor White of Boston. The speaker was a historian of cities, a Bostonian trained at Harvard, and now professor of History and Social Sciences at Boston University.

WE ARE GATHERED this afternoon to pay tribute to those who pledged their lives, fortunes, and honor to create our nation. As we begin the celebration of the two-hundredth anniversary of the founding of the United States of America it would be well to recognize that we have no honor to confer upon the revolutionaries unless we are willing to carry on the tradition they bequeathed to us. We have no honor to confer upon the many men and women who kept alive for us the ideals of 1775 unless we are willing to sustain these ideals in our own lifetimes.

What survives from the Revolution is not a memory, but a tradition. It is a tradition the revolutionaries began, a tradition which successive generations of Americans have nourished and transformed. For us to celebrate the Revolution is to honor not only the men of 1775, but also to recognize the long chain of men and women who have kept alive the vision of a nation of free people.

As a Bostonian I am here to give thanks to the first revolutionaries, the founders, men like John and Sam Adams, Paul Revere, and George Middleton. I am here to give thanks to Elizabeth Blackwell, Lewis Hayden, and William Lloyd Garrison; to Martin Lomasney, David I. Walsh, Elizabeth Peabody; to Louis D. Brandeis, Monroe Trotter, and James Jackson Storrow. The first Revolution sought an independent British Republic of free white men. Later Bostonians joined with their fellow citizens to extend this ideal to include not only the population familiar to an eighteenth-century Briton but also to include newcomers from all over the globe; to include blacks as well as whites; to include women as well as men; to include children as well as adults; to include the poor and the disabled as well as the comfortable and the established. The task is not completed, nor will it ever be.

It is in this spirit of keeping alive the tradition of a nation in search of freedom that I want to contrast the conditions of 1775 with those of our own time. I want to speak of two revolutions: the revolution of the eighteenth century and the revolution of today.

The first revolution was one of the great liberating events of human history; it came as the culmination of more than a century of revolutions, of radical thought and speculation, of institutional innovation. Today we are also in the midst of a revolution, quite literally a turning of things upside down. This time the individual is being forced to the bottom, not raised to the top. Our revolution is also a worldwide event; it afflicts capitalist and socialist nations alike, and it too draws on long historical forces, in this case the forces of nationalism and industrialization.

Our revolution is not an event of human liberation, it is a process of oppression. The power that once resided in the hands of ordinary men and women, the power that was the ultimate safeguard of their liberty, has steadily slipped away from them into the hands of all manner of public and private managers and officials. We are fast becoming, not a beacon of hope for human liberty, but the world's largest exhibit of the corporate society.

We are now a cancerous nation, ever dividing and subdividing into thousands of institutions, public and private. Each institution feeds lustily on the wealth of the nation and the liberties of its citizens. This vigorous growth, however, does not sustain life, it devours it.

In the name of peace it brings us ceaseless wars and prepa-

13

rations for war; in the name of safety it brings us more police and more crime; in the name of free enterprise it brings us fixed prices and monopoly markets; in the name of growth it brings us pollution, economic stagnation, unemployment and underemployment; in the name of social service it brings us schools that don't teach and medicine that does not nourish life; in the name of power to govern it brings us corruption in high places.

I remember being a child in the America of the Great Depression. The country was then, I think, a democracy torn by economic conflict and threatened by Fascist international wars. It was still a democracy. Now I live, like you all, in the world's largest banana republic. We have become since World War II a nation of dodging individuals scurrying to seek safety and security in a world of institutional aggrandizement.

As the men of 1775 took up arms they called themselves the "Sons of Liberty." They called themselves "sons" because they wanted to say that they were men who carried a precious tradition given them by their forefathers. They were the descendants of the English Revolutions of 1640 and 1688, revolutions in which Parliament and the Common Law were raised above the power of kings. They were members of town meetings, congregations, parishes, boroughs, and legislatures; members of institutions of local autonomy which had been slowly evolving over 150 years of Colonial life. Though slaveholders and masters of unfree apprentices and servants, they thought of themselves as a nation of free artisans, shopkeepers, merchants, and farmers. This was their view of the world, and this was the view they wished to preserve and to extend. To do so they were prepared to risk their lives.

In our own time we habitually see ourselves as overwhelmed by newness. It is time we stopped hiding behind the screens of novelty. Let us recall how the men of 1775 used their traditions to cope with revolutionary change. In declaring their independence from Great Britain they rested their hopes upon their established democratic ideas and institutions. They set about to create a new nation of free men by building upon what they knew from the past. They built the Common Law, they adjusted their long-established representative institutions, and they counted upon the wisdom and experience of the ordinary men of the thirteen colonies.

Caught as we are in the powerful net of the twentieth-century corporate revolution, our best hope rests with the same strategy. We must draw upon the democratic institutions and democratic ideals that have grown up among us over the past 200 years. Here, as in 1775, we will find the new sources for our freedom.

Let us look at how the sons and daughters of liberty have been faring in our own time. I am afraid we have been losing our freedom through uncontrolled institutional growth. In our daily business transactions and governmental affairs we have nearly consumed our heritage. The corporate revolution has been a noiseless revolution; it feeds on the mundane activities of everyday life.

Like all major social events the corporate revolution compounds the new with the old. Since World War II an unprecedented prosperity has swept the nation. Americans have enjoyed a remarkable increase in real income. This income has been consumed in the form of more goods and services, in the form of shorter hours, and in the form of the diversion of millions of young people from the work force into schools and colleges.

Such changes inevitably unleashed new demands and new expectations. Workers have expected better conditions on the job; parents and children better schools; husbands and wives, armed with the new leisure, expected a richer family life. Prosperity touched every avenue of the society. It was all quite natural; new wealth always creates the tensions of new

15

possibilities as yet unrealized. New visions of personal freedoms for blacks, for women, for workers, for students arose at the very moment when institutionalization ate away the old freedoms.

This new wealth, however, was not distributed in new ways. It followed the economic ordering of American society that has prevailed at least since the eighteenth century. A much larger share of the added increment went to the well-to-do than to low-income Americans. No important shift in the income shares of our population has accompanied the new prosperity. We remain, as always, a nation 30 percent poor, 60 percent middle class, and 10 percent rich.

It is the way we work which has changed more than anything else since World War II. To an extraordinary degree we have become a nation of institutions and of institutional workers. Government employment embraces more and more of the nation's work — especially state and local government and the federal military. Institutional jobs in schools, hospitals, and social services have grown the fastest. They exceed the rapid bureaucratization of the lives of men and women in sales, clerical, and manufacturing employment.[1]

---

1. From 1946 to 1970 nonagricultural employment has changed as follows. In 1946 manufacturing accounted for 34 percent; wholesaling, retailing, services, finance, insurance, and real estate for 33.5 percent; all-government civilian employment for 13.6 percent. In 1970 manufacturing was down to 27.4 percent; wholesaling, retailing, services, finance, insurance, and real estate up to 42.8 percent; and government up to 17.8 percent.

In 1970 among private employees covered by Social Security 50.6 percent worked in establishments, that is, work places, of 100 or more employees.

Federal government employment has been steady since World War II. There were 2,434,000 civilian employees in 1946, 2,881,000 in 1970. State and local employment has flourished: state employment up from 804,000 employees in 1946 to 2,755,000 in 1970; local employment up from 2,762,000 in 1946 to 7,392,000 in 1970.

The armed forces on active duty have doubled in the same interval, from 1,587,000 after demobilization in 1947 to 3,066,000 in 1970 during the Vietnam war. All statistics are from the U.S. Bureau of the Census, *Historical Statistics of the United States,* and the *1971 Statistical Abstract of the U.S.*

As the latest stage in this process the corporation is now reaching out into farming.

It is from these three massive ingredients — the new wealth, the unchanging income distribution, and the growing institutionalization — that the corporate revolution has been forged. We have the habit of celebrating prosperity in America. But we seldom look at the way that wealth is created. We do not look at the changes in the daily relationships among people which are determined by the ways our nation creates its wealth. It is the way we treat each other as we earn our livings and pay our wages that is the source of oppression in our new corporate world. Let us look at how each of the major divisions of our society is faring — the poor, the middle classes, and the rich.

First, to be poor in America today means to be poor in the midst of an incredibly wealthy society. This is a new situation which we must all come to understand. These are not the days of the Model T and the outhouse, the cold-water flat, and the smell of oil heaters. Our memories of a simpler America are not reliable guides to the present. The only historical precedents we have for the present condition of our low-income population are house servants and poor relations. The cook eating the leftovers in the kitchen and the widowed cousin shivering in the cold back room, these are the analogies of today's poor in the midst of plenty.

The urban riots and angry confrontations of a few years ago were demands for recognition, calls for dignity and equity. The left-out, the ignored, the pushed-aside wanted to be included in our society as full-fledged members of the family.

The American poor are not the same group they once were. They are not strangers among us, not country folks, not young men from overseas. They are mostly long-resident Americans, even long-resident city dwellers. Many are old, many young women and children. They don't have to learn our culture, they are products of it. Their expectations have been formed by the disciplines of today's urban life: high rents, low wages, and unemployment. They have been trained to expect little of themselves and little of their society, with jobs their employers do not respect, low wages, and insecurity, which do not even let them find dignity as consumers. The children are similarly trained by the city's schools and the city's streets.

Even though the poor have little cash with which to attract the custom of modern corporations, they have been institutionalized. But their institutions are different from ours. We know them all: the housing project, the hospital, the social agency, the welfare office, the slum school. They are the subjects of everyday's newspaper. The story is always the same. It is a tale of the dehumanizing and demeaning interactions between the client poor and their institutional caretakers.

To assume their places as full-fledged American citizens, to escape these bureaucrats, the poor need jobs, and they need jobs which will enable each worker to support his or her family at a level the rest of us see as decent, dignified, and independent.

The great middle classes of America — the regularly employed, well-paid blue- and white-collar workers — also have serious economic problems these days. They suffer from layoffs, cutbacks, job insecurity, too many debts, and losses in real income from inflation. These problems of a mismanaged economy must be attended to, and I think they will be, somehow.

The way these needs are addressed, however, is a crucial issue for the future of a free society. In the past each rescue operation performed upon the economy has hastened the corporate revolution. The New Deal, the Fair Deal, the Great Society, and their Republican alternates have all driven bureaucracy deeper into our daily lives. Compared to the poor, the middle-income Americans have reaped substantial economic benefits from our public programs, but the cost to the middle classes incurred by these changes has been enormous. Their work and family life have been transformed. They have lost control over their jobs, their families, their government, and their environment.

The biggest benefactors of our economic management have been the public and private corporations of the nation. Historically the corporate revolution moved up through the middle classes, from the artisans to the professionals. Large-scale enterprise came first to manufacturing, transportation, and finance; then to government, services, and commerce. The course of unionization tells the story: the long struggles of artisans, factory workers, and railroadmen for unionization moved in our own time into government, hospitals, schools, universities, and white-collar work in general.

With large-scale enterprise came subtle and pervasive new methods of social control. Small things multiplied to become new webs of power and discipline. The early twentieth-century invention of cost accounting and time budget has matured into computerized production, sales, and inventory controls; supply cages for tools have become requisitions and purchase orders; administrators and supervisors multiply to maintain direction and formal communications; and to an extraordinary degree TV and electronic surveillance bespeak the new relationships between employer and employee. The loss of autonomy and dignity that these changes signal for the middle class find expression in vernacular phrases like "channels," "paper," and "chicken." I don't hear a demand from the middle classes to run our giant enterprises or government offices. Perhaps that will come. For the present what the middle classes want is more to say about how they do the work they must do.

The basic tasks of middle-class family life have not altered with the years. Money must be found, children raised, sickness provided for now as always. But the paths these families must follow through the society have changed enormously. The old difficulties are not the new ones. In the past, middle-class Americans sought some measure of autonomy within the disciplines of economic life by mastering a craft or a profession or by establishing a small business. They sought escape and some leverage against the society by the purchase of a home, accumulation of some savings.

Now they must play the game of bureaucratic mobility. One must move up the organizational ladder to attain seniority, tenure, job security, a pension; one must move up to pay for ever-more elaborate education for the children, so they can start as high up as possible on a similar ladder. It is a demanding game, often as cruel, confining, and severe in its way as the old property race which preceded it. It is no less demanding than the past because, as the income figures show, there is proportionately as much poverty and as little room at the top now as there was thirty or sixty years ago.

Till recent years the family was the great escape and the central motive in the lives of our middle classes. Today both children and adults are totally enmeshed in the new institutionalism. As never before the wives are committed to wage labor. Most middle-class families depend on their women's earnings for their standard of living. Indeed, working wives and mothers have often been the only access to post–World War II prosperity. Middle-class family life no longer offers, as it seemed to in the "togetherness era" of the fifties, an escape from the strains of bureaucratic life. Father, mother, and child go daily to an institution, where they must conform, or find another institution. The reports from the middle classes on these changes have been remarkably consistent since World War II. We have seen their reactions on television, but we have not responded to them. We do not respond because we do not see the connections between their traps and our own.

Divorce courts also give a measure of the pressures on the family. The divorce rate of 43.6 percent of current marriages (in 1974 there were 2,223,000 marriages, 970,000 divorces) is a sign that this one institution is carrying more weight than it can bear. Whether you see this trend as a progressive transition toward new forms of domestic life, or as a social disaster, we must all agree that something vital is happening at the center of American life.

Consider, too, the agenda of the women's liberation movement, the demands of radical local unions, and the insights and experiments now going on with Catholic and Protestant churches and Oriental sects. All are movements of the middle classes, all tell the same tale — the fragmentation of daily life, the absence of personal autonomy and dignity, the illegitimate use of authority, the bankruptcy of individual striving unless it is expressed in some social context which holds a wider human meaning than personal aggrandizement. Wholeness, dignity, and autonomy within meaningful groups are the demands common to these extraordinary diverse responses to our bureaucratic society. Control of the new corporate America is the inescapable task for America's middle classes.

The rich and the powerful have not been ignorant of these changes or unaware of new demands. Yet I see no conspiracy of power. Rather I see separate clusters of power, each assessing the situation by the logic of its own advantage. Though divided among themselves, leaders in government, business, labor, and philanthropy have steadily supported a series of in stitutional innovations they hoped would meet the new social conditions. But these reforms were not allowed to alter the trend toward institutional growth. For the urban poor there has been a steady stream of institutional innovations in education, health, housing, welfare, social services, and police. But these piecemeal efforts have left untouched the job, income, and housing problems of the poor and have failed to secure the safety and social order of the city.

The rich and powerful meet the middle classes on a day-to-day basis; they are the immediate employees. Their responses to institutionalization have been remarkably uniform, although they have in no way been organized class actions. On the job they express their helplessness with sloth, foot-dragging, inefficiency, surliness, irresponsibility, and as dead wood. More unexpectedly conflicts with institutionalization have appeared among children as delinquency, disorder, and apathy in the schools, the suburbs, and the universities.

To counter this loss in morale among the middle classes, the upper class has set in motion remedies appropriate to a bureaucratic world. No leader in business, labor, government, philanthropy, or social service has proposed altering the power relationships that are poisoning our institutional life. Instead, machines have been substituted for men wherever possible; more administrators and more supervisors have been hired where machines could not do the work of people; counselors and social workers have been added to quiet schools and suburbs. Where open rebellion broke out they sent police, secret police, provocative agents, and the National Guard. There were killings at colleges in Ohio and Mississippi and mass arrests in Washington, D.C. The CIA, the FBI, the NSA, and Watergate represent the end of this line. They are the very antithesis of everything the first American Revolution stood for. They are the betrayal of our heritage by our fellow sons and daughters of liberty.

These extreme political actions are dramatic signs of new circumstances of everyday life in America. The upper class has gathered more and more formal power into the hands of our public and private institutions and has concentrated that power at the bureaucratic peak of these institutions. There are more and more layers between the decision-makers and the objects of their decisions. Lower-class poverty and disorder is unabated. The middle classes, after a decade of open rebellion, are now quiet and fearful, but they persist in their disengaged and escapist ways.

The path away from this corporate dead end will not be easy to find nor easy to negotiate. The corporate revolution reaches so deeply into all aspects of our society, and feeds on such powerful historical forces, that dramatic changes in power relationships must be made. We will have to face and solve issues of the control and allocation of natural resources, the control and allocation of the accumulated wealth of the nation, the management of private corporations and all manner of public institutions, and the rights of individuals and small groups, not only in the neighborhoods, but especially in the work places themselves.

Unlike the situation at the time of the first revolution, we have today no evolving traditions of the English Common Law, no succession of revolutions in advanced countries, no slow evolution of local institutions and local economies to suggest the path we should take to regain control of our lives. At present we do not have alternatives to our corporations, and even our academics have yet to specify a new way. All we have is a thirty-year record of protests and small experiments.

But we do have a common tradition and a common understanding with which to confront our plight. We have the tradition of our first revolution and its goals of dignity and freedom.

I propose that we use these next two Bicentennial years to strengthen that tradition by addressing ourselves to the present condition of liberty in America. As a first step I urge you to go home and think about the present constraints on your liberties. I urge you, by yourself or with your friends, to draw up a petition for the restoration or enlargement of your᷀ liberties, and to send that document to your representatives in state and federal government.

In their constant alarms over war, and their daily attendance on the pressures and counterpressures of powerful groups, our leaders behave as if they had no sense of what it is like for most who live in America today. They seem to have no sense of what it means to be a son or daughter of liberty in 1975. It's time we told them once again.

Let me conclude by offering you an example, my own petition for the restoration of my liberties and those of other Americans. I do not propose a new society, but a few ways in which we can use our democratic tradition and democratic institutions to bring the corporate revolution under control.

As I see it we need the strength, work, and wisdom of all American citizens: we must open up our corporate world to public scrutiny and public experiment; we must increase the power of our citizens over their local institutions and government and labor; and we must liberate them from secret police; we must liberate our cultural institutions from the class advantage they now labor under so that they can address the problems, experiences, and feelings of everyday American life.

First, every American adult must be given a job and paid a living wage. Until this condition is met we do not have a nation of citizens. We must complete the historic process of expanding our effective citizenry that was begun in 1775.

I do not want to sentimentalize the circumstances of our first revolution. Boston in 1775 was no democratic Garden of Eden. There were many who believed in sharp distinctions in wealth, power, and privilege. There were unfree servants, traders in black slaves. There were rum shops, prostitutes, and violent street gangs. But there were no leftover people. If a man wanted work, he could find work, and by working he could support himself and his family according to the standards of decency for his day.

One thing is clear. Boston was not then, as it is now, a giant factory for the manufacture of left-out people. It was not a place whose schools, streets, and shops turned out people no one respected or had a place for. There were no long lines of unemployed or people waiting for unemployment checks. It was not a city, or a part of a nation, in which one could spend a lifetime working and never make enough money to support one's family according to the standards of decency of the majority.

We have the resources to see that every American has a decent job and a living wage. The means are at hand in public employment, in tax reform, and in cuts in military expenditures. By taking such steps we can at last become a nation of free, dignified, and contributing citizens.

Second, the idea of the permanent corporation must be modified so that all our public and private institutions are subject to periodic review. No public or private corporation or trust, or combination of such entities, should be granted the privilege of existence forever without regular examination of its usefulness and its performance. At the end of a limited time — say forty years to start off the discussion — every corporation in the United States should be required to justify continuance of its charter, or failing public approval it must close down and distribute its assets or come under different management.

Nothing in the principles of the first revolution, or in our subsequent traditions as a nation of free people, requires that we grant the right to establish private dynasties or perpetual institutions. Indeed the first revolutionaries set a wise precedent for us. No constitution was written without provision for its amendment. The revolutionaries abolished primogeniture and entail and seized the great manors and colonial proprietorships. In that agricultural era such feudal privileges threatened the same kind of massive encapsulation of power as our corporations now create in an industrial age.

The question of due representation of capital, management, labor, and the consumer in the governance of corporations is now a vexed issue around the world. The needs and goals of institutions vary enormously. A steel mill is not like a hospital, or a transit authority. Legislation and administrative regulations governing each type of activity and institution will have to be developed. In some years these will be wise, useful, and enduring. In others they will be foolish, even corrupt. Sometimes we will balance the needs of capital, labor, management, and the consumer; sometimes we will not. Yet in the long range, as we begin afresh with each corporation, an adequate American style will emerge by trial and error.

Eighty-five years of federal regulation of business, and eighty-five years of antitrust laws, have proved no protection against the institutionalization of our nation. We have harassed some businessmen and prospered many lawyers but have not succeeded in protecting the worker, the consumer, or our national resources. Now even our capital is in jeopardy. Periodic review would prevent no one from realizing the dream of building a giant enterprise. If after forty years, say, General Motors does not meet our needs, it is time someone else had a chance to build automobiles.

Third, corporate records must be made public documents, available to all. Corporations, public, private, and philanthropic, must be subject to full disclosure laws on penalty of losing their charters. We cannot learn to cope with our corporate society unless we can monitor the decisions that so powerfully affect our lives.

Fourth, local governments must be given the resources necessary to deal with local problems. The access of our citizens to the taxable wealth of our society must no longer depend on the patterns of class and racial segregation and the fortunes of the real estate market. By statewide taxation of property, income, and sales, and by per-capita budgeting we can restore to the city, to the town, and to the county the power to manage its own affairs. To delay such tax equalization is to continue to undermine local government in America.

Fifth, local labor unions must be guaranteed the right to bargain and to strike over local conditions, regardless of any national union-management contracts. If union democracy is to be preserved and industrial democracy fostered, it is essential that the powers of the locals be safeguarded.

Sixth, all secret police must be abolished and private surveillance of all kinds must be stopped. Secret police and spying poison the wells of social and political innovation. The historical record of our secret police is clear enough. First instituted during World War I and perpetuated as the FBI and numerous later institutions, such police have not made us more safe at work or at home. Instead they have added their own crimes to those of the private society. They have consistently been used to crush dissenting groups. We may not enjoy all aspects of a free society, a society which includes both the Klan and the Weathermen, but such a society is infinitely safer for the individual and much more socially creative than the incipient police state we now have.

We need also to dismantle the system of private spying and of file dossiers that business and government have established. We learned during the McCarthy era of the abuses of credit records and government files. The central intelligence of a credit card society is not necessary for our economic prosperity. By a thoughtless pursuit of mass consumer credit and social and political conformity we have breached the legitimate boundaries of privacy of our citizens and our political officials.

Seventh, and finally, federal, state, and local tax exemptions for educational, philanthropic, religious, and other nonprofit institutions should be withdrawn, and research grants to such institutions should be drastically reduced. The nonprofit secular and religious institutions of America have become the established churches, chantries, and monastaries that the Sons of Liberty and their forefathers disestablished. Let us complete their work.

The person who prays with the sick, the researcher who seeks the cause of the disease, the school that trains the doctor are no more, and no less, worthy than the person who gives useful employment and decent wages to his fellow citizens. Let each flourish among us, but let us not make one bear the burdens of civil society while others do not. Let us not establish a privileged caste of the mind.

For example, the current federal income tax exemption for charitable donations alone amounts to a subsidy of more than three billion dollars annually. Like most other tax exemptions it favors the rich and underwrites the gift of the wealthy over that of the ordinary citizen. If one adds these class effects of taxation to the cultural effects of direct subsidies for research and the arts, the consequences add up to a social disaster.

After World War II, at the very moment when the corporate pace of our national life grew ever more rapid, we began to pour millions of dollars into research which hastened the institutionalization of our cultural life. The result has been to buy up a whole generation of our most highly trained minds and to set them to work at mandarin tasks, tasks far removed from the needs of the general society, its life, and its culture.

Even today our most lively congregations are not those of churches bound to heavy real estate investments; our most innovative campuses are not those with the greatest research budgets; our most creative artists and writers are not those "in residence." Let us disestablish our religious and cultural institutions, for their own sakes as well as ours. At no time in our history have we been in greater need of the free and liberated energies of our native spirit.

Such then, is my own personal petition for the restoration of our liberties. It by no means exhausts the possible public actions which might be taken to deal with the corporate revolution. It attempts only to call your attention to the plight in which we find ourselves. It seeks to open debate on the essential facts.

If this petition seems extreme to you, let me remind you that the modern corporation, the modern labor union, indeed the United States itself were all innovations that grew slowly from the needs and possibilities of daily life in the past. In our new urban and corporate nation we must find the sources of our freedoms where we have always found them — in the dignity, power, and wisdom of ordinary American citizens.

Questions and Discussion

THE DOWNTOWN AUDIENCE

The audience was a mixture of business and professional men and their wives, members of neighborhood groups, old residents and new. The Boston-lovers were there, the history enthusiasts, and a sprinkling of officials who attend public ceremonies. There were also a few radicals, who perhaps hoped to use the Bicentennial for their own ends.

The audience was sharply divided over the address, some shocked, others enthusiastic, and they responded with a mixture of coldness and concern. Three gentlemen of mercantile appearance had walked out. When the questions were handed up from the floor most were responses to the plea for a more just America. Was it possible? How could it be achieved? The feeling most often expressed was a sense of powerlessness, of not being able to find an entering wedge to separate and attack the problems of modern society. The question took many forms:

What can we do to gain greater control of our world?

Will Americans have the courage to demand the changes the speaker asks for?

The vision of an America of renewed individual freedom is appealing. But will it require even more bureaucracy than we have now?

And there were voices of dissent:

How much was the first revolution motivated by democratic ideals and how much by materialism and commercial interest?

Given the difference in population then and now, is institutionalization really greater than it was 200 years ago?

Would corporations suffer the loss of perpetuity without violence? Should they?

If the audience shared a common feeling, perhaps it was expressed by one who asked, "cannot a new ethic, new liberty, and new meaning be injected into corporate life?

DISCUSSION AT PARKMAN HOUSE

That evening a group of invited guests [2] gathered for dinner and discussion at the Parkman House, another civic symbol. A mansion near the crest of Beacon Hill, overlooking Boston Common, it was built in 1824 and was given to the city by the

2. Present were Kevin H. White, Mayor of Boston; Abram T. Collier, Chairman, New England Mutual Life Insurance Company; Ronald Edmonds, Director, Center for Urban Studies, Harvard School of Education; Pauline Harrell, attorney, Director, Victorian Society; John Howe, President, Provident Institution for Savings; Katherine Kane, Director, Boston 200; David Kunze, engineer, President, Roslindale Historical Society; Sander Levin, Fellow, Kennedy

Parkman family in 1908. In 1973 it was splendidly restored as a guest house for distinguished visitors, and parts of it were converted into an urban conference center.

The evening discussion revealed a similar split in opinion but took a more philosophical turn than it had in the afternoon. All agreed that in a huge nation of megalopolitan complexes, elaborate technology, and international commerce, large public and private institutions were inevitable. But some thought our citizens are socially mobile and our institutions open and responsive, while others saw inequality among the people and constraints and irresponsibility in our institutions.

The first group saw this country as unique, a place of personal freedom and unequaled opportunity. Here, they felt, a high standard of living sustains millions, and power is wielded with considerable sensitivity to the needs and demands of the public. The problems of the nation, this group believed, come from the imperfections in its political arrangements and more particularly from recent failures of its national government.

The other group stressed the conflicts between the ideal of individual freedom and the constraints imposed by big government, big cities, and big business. The present structure of our society, these people felt, fosters bureaucratic hierarchies and rewards a few at the expense of the many. Given the extent of the national wealth too many Americans are poor, and too much human damage is done by the present patterns of work and domestic life. For this group the recent failures of the federal government were themselves products of large-scale organization.

Institute of Politics, Harvard University; Ian Menzies, editorial writer, Boston *Globe*; S. M. Miller, Chairman, Department of Sociology, Boston University; David L. Rosenbloom, Executive Assistant to the Mayor of Boston; Edward Schwartz, Institute for the Study of Civic Values, Philadelphia; Sam Bass Warner, Jr., Professor of History and Social Science, Boston University.

The first group saw in today's America a continuation of Jefferson's open society, the benign aristocracy of talent. The second group contrasted the circumstances of the ordinary city dweller with the dignity and independence of Jefferson's farmers. This polarity, already present among the factions that made up the American Revolution, seems two centuries later to be basic in our democratic tradition. Polar views provide lenses through which Americans judge their everyday experience and frame their hopes for the future.

Debate about how far government was separated from public sentiment opened up the core philosophical difference among the discussants. One who thought government was responding to new conditions, even if slowly, argued, "I don't think our leaders have lost all sense of what it is like to live in America today. That makes it look as if we just need to change leaders and everything will be all right. I think our problems lie much deeper, that the nation faces dramatically new conditions so it is no wonder leaders fail. We are a nation of 200 million; in 1900 of only 75 million. We have changed profoundly just through urbanization and the loss of elbow room."

Those who opposed the view that America is moving toward its goal of a free and open society held that the main problem was a basic failure in the values and institutions of our political tradition. The liberal tradition holds that it is possible to infuse justice into the present economic order: that if we create enough wealth in the country, there will be something for everyone. It wouldn't matter then that we have 30 percent poor, 60 percent middle class, and 10 percent rich. The poor would be rich enough.

Opponents of this liberal view felt that it ignores both the idea of dignity and the logic of corporate, technological, and economic investment. For example, if there is a conflict between taxes on corporations and supporting the schools, we lower the taxes that pay for the schools. That is how liberalism works.

In the final dialogue of the evening the two main strands of opinion about American social and political tradition were fully and clearly separated.

"Our tradition goes much farther back than the American Revolution," one speaker began. "Farther than the English Revolution, it goes back to the Golden Age of Greece and according to that tradition most of the institutions that make up the American social order are grotesque.

"Thomas Jefferson preferred the country and farming people because he believed they possessed virtues he esteemed and eloquently described. He said that when you see the smoke from your neighbor's chimney it is time to move on. He meant by this that there is something about the human spirit that will not tolerate crowding, being regimented or regulated. Not only must we have room in which to exercise our individuality, we must have room of all kinds — physical, intellectual, emotional — in which to be ourselves.

"Jefferson's ideas, in the context of today, mean that we ought to see how much room there is in our prevailing institutions for exercising all those qualities most admirable in the human condition. I share the speaker's alarm about the fact that in most important senses we are too crowded to survive in a way which makes surviving worth while."

Finally, a business executive and author of a prize-winning book on management saw all the previous discussion as based on the view that America was divided into classes. Though the speakers had drawn different conclusions, he felt they had missed what was to him a central fact of American life: its openness, the mobility among levels of income and status, not the levels themselves. As he explained his views there emerged a classic defense of modern America as an open society.

"All the things that have been said tonight are on the same wavelength. You are saying that we have a class structure here in America. I grew up on a farm, went to a high school where there were twenty people in my class. I considered myself to be a member of the working class. Then when I got through college I began to consider myself as belonging to the middle class. In recent years I've been told that I am part of the 10 percent, the upper class — that I have power, control. And yet I perceive America today, more than any other society I know in history, as being an open society even with all its restrictions and its limitations.

"Our ideals for human development and human dignity have been far greater than our accomplishments. Our ideals are still there, thank God, but I think that when we talk about institutions and institutionalization we have to realize that we are dealing with a society not of 200 thousand but of more than 200 million people, in a world of over three billion, where to accomplish things we have to organize. In this country we have tried to do so, as much as possible, within the context of freedom.

"The other side of the coin of freedom is always discipline, and it is hoped self-discipline, that is, voluntary compliance with the public law and with the private law of the organization with which you associate yourself. When we talk about institutions we mistake things very badly if we fail to realize that institutions are people. In the last generation or two the leaders of most of our institutions have become, despite their words, very sensitive to the fact that their authority does not lie in ownership or control, but comes from people — from the customers who are willing to do business with them, from the employees who are willing to stay with them, and from their own competence in bringing people together to do things."

So was the spectrum of opinion rounded out.

THE RADIO AUDIENCE

"The Two Revolutions" was broadcast over National Public Radio Sunday, February 16, and was followed by an hour-and-a-half question period in which listeners phoned questions and responses to a moderator and a panel of discussants.[3]

With this audience the address raised two main kinds of questions, both with a practical slant: first, how could private corporations be controlled by the time-limited charter proposal? Second, what can the individual citizen do to improve society?

Among those concerned about the practicality of the time-limited charter, one thought it would disrupt the continuity of management and the teamwork of employees. Another asked how a giant like General Motors could be subjected to possible dissolution without destroying the auto industry and with it the national economy. A third believed that bureaucratization was inevitable and could not be controlled.

Professor Warner answered these questions in some detail:

"Let's first be clear on the proposal itself. What we are looking for is a self-operating device to make our institutions come forward periodically for public review. If charters expire automatically we will not have to depend on the alertness of bureaucratic regulators.

"We are also looking for a legal way for the nation to experiment with modes of governing its large institutions without regulating solely from the outside or nationalizing large segments of the economy. Regulation, in use since 1890, has proved cumbersome and ineffective. Nationalization has

---

3. The moderator was Sander Vanocur, in Washington, D.C., Edward Schwartz in Philadelphia, and Sam Bass Warner, Jr., in Boston. It will be remembered that Schwartz was one of the discussants at the Parkman House Seminar.

created unwieldy bureaucracies in the socialist states that have used it extensively. We would impose on the corporation internal changes from time to time, and periodic review of its managerial performance. The most likely event, when a charter expired, would be a review and the issuing of a revised charter.

"Since we want supervision at the scale of modern enterprise, we would have to shift from state to federal incorporation. The rules would be set forth in a general statute, amended from time to time as we gained experience with corporate forms and alternate costs and benefits. The basic law would deal with the representation of stockholders, employees, consumers, and perhaps public interest in the corporation. The law would also bring together all current regulations worth continuing.

"Federal review boards, in public hearings on charter applications, would deal with two issues: Does the charter conform with existing statutes? And does the past performance of the proposed management (directors and company officers) suggest future behavior that would meet public standards? Evidence of illegal practices, violations of business law, illegal political contributions, bribery, fraud, corporate looting, or failure to meet some minimum level of business competence would be looked for and weighed. I think the Penn Central Railroad, some years ago, and ITT would be denied new charters under this process. What we seek is some public accountability for corporate managers just as we are trying to find ways to make public administrators and bureaucracies accountable for their performance.

"Consider the stockholders, directors, and officers of a successful corporation on the eve of its charter's expiration. It is hard to see them asking to be dissolved. Rather, they would propose a charter that conformed to the law, and they would prepare for federal review according to the rules. The normal businessman would have little trouble standing on his record.

"What would be novel, and important, is the review itself. It would force managers and owners to recognize the public responsibility of economic office."

Panel and audience then moved to other concerns. "We have no one to appeal to," said a lady from Utah, "no one in government or in law enforcement, and no real access to the media except on rare occasions such as tonight. We feel total impotence all round."

Edward Schwartz, one of the panelists, replied that people in Philadelphia feel the same way. He continued: "We have been organizing working people in neighborhoods to fight for a fairer shake in the wealth of the country, and for things we need as communities. We started a group called the Tea Party, for tax reform. We now have a thousand members, we are organized in every congressional district in the city, and we have a lot of power in the state. We are putting a lot of pressure on some of our congressmen to go after the oil industry and to close tax loopholes.

"Now that's the old American process of democratic organizing. But most of our institutions don't encourage it. We go to school and we are told we shouldn't be political. If we start talking politics we must be very quiet and we must not organize. I think the revolution needed in America now is one to create politics where politics is forbidden."

A man in Texas raised the painful issue of racism in American cities. "In Austin there are people who call themselves Americans to Restore Freedom. They want to keep their communities closed so that whole categories of people will be left out — out of the schools, out of the neighborhoods, and out of the work places. How do we argue with our neighbors in favor of opening up our communities so nobody is left out?"

Schwartz also shed light on this problem. "If you have two people, one doesn't like the other, and you want to get them together, you have to convince the hostile person that the other agrees with him on a lot of important things. Right now black people and whites agree that this economy is out of control and that it is run by rich people and corporations. There are a lot of opportunities to build alliances. Blacks and whites fight together for tax reform. When they work together on common goals that have nothing to do with blackness or whiteness, they can see beyond race."

A woman in Wisconsin was alarmed at the falling rate of voter participation in elections. A Colorado man felt that public alienation was turning inward into mounting anger, which might be mobilized by an unscrupulous government for the support of another foreign war.

The discussion ended on a timely question about the effects of the current depression on long-term goals. Professor Warner answered that the many people who are unhappy about jobs and income will bring together coalitions among unionized workers, poor blacks, poor whites, and middle-class people of all kinds. So it will be possible again to build a coalition around economic interests that should be met by government. "I can see," he concluded, "the current depression producing a first step in our coming together."

Schwartz saw government as laggard in understanding the national mind. "Most people favor a huge public-service job program. The government is not responding to that wish. Most people want gas rationing, not energy taxes. The government is not responding to that wish. Most people favor tax reform and the closing of loopholes that give corporations subsidies of billions. They have favored tax reform for years, and government is not responding to that wish. The big issue is whether government is going to respond to what every poll shows is the will of the people."

Big government and big corporations were taking away many of the freedoms our original revolution had given us.

3

The Rights of Man

CHARLES E. WYZANSKI, JR.

It was something of a civic holiday when Judge Charles E. Wyzanski, Jr., delivered his address "The Rights of Man" on April 16,
1975. Nature offered a warm spring afternoon. The weekend
promised the Patriot's Day parades and the reenactment of the
Battle of Concord and Lexington that Bostonians yearly enjoy, and
this spring brought the added festivity of the national Bicentennial
and a visit from President Ford.

As the downtown audience streamed into Faneuil Hall those who
knew Judge Wyzanski looked forward to an oration of some formal-
ity and elegance. The judge spoke for an hour extempore, completely without notes. His strong voice and his obvious command
of his argument bore his listeners along on a tide of assurance. He
was tradition itself, calling to mind James Otis, Daniel Webster,
and others who had made history in that hall.

A Bostonian by birth, Judge Wyzanski graduated from Phillips
Exeter Academy in 1923, received his B.A. degree, magna cum
laude, from Harvard in 1927 and his LL.B., magna cum laude, in
1930. He served as law secretary to U.S. Circuit Judges Augustus
N. Hand and Learned Hand, has been for many years a U.S. District judge, has held numerous government posts, was president of

the Board of Overseers of Harvard University, and has been a trustee of the Ford Foundation since 1951.

MR. COLLIER, thank you for that very handsome introduction and for the diligent research of my past, including a speech which I delivered forty years ago to an Exeter gathering.

Mr. Mayor, I am complimented that you were willing to come to hear a Federal District Judge. I had not known that you were so willing to come within the jurisdiction of the Federal Court. You, as mayor, have national prominence not only because of your personal character and quality, but also because the nation is focused on this city. It includes Boston Harbor, where the tea was dumped and Charlestown, where Bunker Hill was fought, and also South Boston and Roxbury which, were it not for a stable Mayor, might have started a second American Revolution.

As I came from the mayor's office with the mayor and the company you see on this platform, we went by the statue of Samuel Adams, born and resident for many years, on Purchase Street, around the corner. It was on the second of November in 1774 that Samuel Adams, at a meeting of the authorities of Boston, moved that there should be Committees of Correspondence which should circulate through every town in the Commonwealth and beyond, through the Colonies as a whole, a statement of the Rights of Man.

I suppose it must have been to some extent that experience which led someone — neither the mayor, nor Mr. Collier, nor myself — to select as the title for my talk, "The Rights of Man." As Mr. Collier has indicated, this has not been in all quarters regarded as a very happy selection.

Eleanor Roosevelt in 1948, when she presided at the United Nations Commission on Human Rights, was ill-advised enough to suggest that the first article in the proposed Declaration of Human Rights should be taken directly from the Declaration of Independence and should read, "All *men* are created equal." She soon learned that there would be an international protest, and the first article now reads, "All *people* are created equal."

But, of course, we may be forgiven for using as a title on any Bicentennial occasion the phrase, "the Rights of Man," for that was indeed, historically, a wholly correct description of the doctrines as they were advocated in the eighteenth century.

Thomas Paine's book on this topic is still widely known. Indeed, phraseology using much the same language exists in Virginia, in the Massachusetts constitution, and in the French Declaration of Rights. So in many countries the phrase would be understood, as I hope it is understood by this audience, as referring not to men as a gender, but to men as a species, as human beings.

To talk in Faneuil Hall on this occasion is bound to make those of us who remember James Otis feel how appropriate the place is. It was here, in this very room, in 1763 that James Otis delivered the third of his series of remarkable speeches which centered on the rights of British subjects and, in that sense, the rights of man.

It was not here, of course, that he argued the case involving the writs of assistance. That was in 1761 at the State House. But it is here that he gave utterance to sentiments which led Lord Acton in his *Lectures On the French Revolution* to quote John Adams to the effect that every important idea in the Declaration of Independence and every important argument which was advocated to justify the Revolution may be found in James Otis' speeches here.

I have a special, additional reason to be glad to speak in Faneuil Hall. It's the first time I've spoken here. But my wife has spoken here earlier, and now I'm trying to catch up.

In talking tonight on the Rights of Man, I am going to summarize elliptically the origins of the doctrines. Then I am going to survey briefly 200 years of experience with respect to the doctrines. Finally, I am going to take a look at what seems to me to be the prospect.

People may differ as to where the ideas of the Rights of Man originated. Classical scholars might not agree, but lawyers like Professor Lauterpacht of Cambridge University would have traced the Rights of Man to the views of the ancient Greeks with respect to what we call, but they did not call, "natural law."

One can find in the arguments between Antigone and Creon, in Sophocles' play, ideas which certainly are akin to some of those which are found in Declarations of Rights of Man. And if one reads in a rather unhistorical way the Funeral Speech of Pericles, there are phrases which would have seemed congenial to the eighteenth-century patriots who stood for the Declaration of the Rights of Man. But I think most people would say that the principal sources of the Declaration of the Rights of Man were the writings of John Locke and of, the less well-known to our generation, Algernon Sidney.

It is no accident that the first mayor of Boston, the distinguished predecessor of our distinguished chairman, Josiah Quincy, came of a family in which we know that there was a specific legacy from father to son of the books of Locke and Sidney, because it was felt by the testator that any person who would be concerned with the civic obligations of this community should know those writings.

One, of course, recognizes that many of the Founding Fathers knew something of French writings by Rousseau and Montesquieu and Voltaire. They knew something of Beccaria and Bodin. But it is a little doubtful whether what they knew was firsthand, except in the case of as learned a person as Thomas Jefferson.

In addition to the sources which were classical, and philosophic, and Continental, one must in truth say that there is a much greater debt than is sometimes recognized to the law. Bernard Bailyn, a current professor of distinction at Harvard, has written, and received prizes for, a book on the *Ideological Origins Of The American Revolution;* and he, after careful analysis, comes to the conclusion that many of the ideas which are associated with the doctrines of the Rights of Man are indeed doctrines which reached our Founding Fathers through the medium of the law. What better indication could there be than the speeches of James Otis himself? For when James Otis argued against the validity of the writs of assistance, after arguing that they were contrary to the statutes, he said that they were contrary to the principles of natural law as set forth in Coke and in Sir Matthew Hale, two English judges.

Moreover, it has always been perceived that the lawyers as a class were among the most effective agitators who led to the American Revolution.

In any case, as we all very well know, the form in which the Rights of Man is best remembered by all of us is in the Declaration of Independence.

I would not be so vain as to try to trace the pedigree of that. Carl Becker did it better than anyone else will ever do it again. But on June 12, 1776, in Virginia, there was a state Declaration of Rights, and that document was, of course, before the men in Philadelphia the next month.

All of us know at least some of the phrases of the Declaration of Independence, and thus know something about the doctrines of the Rights of Man. We do not need to be reminded that it is from there that we have such phrases as "all men are created equal." We know that the phrases with respect to the unalienable rights to life, liberty, and the pursuit of happiness come from that document. And we are aware that there is repeated the idea that governments are created by men and are to serve the purposes of men. Moreover, *there* is the idea of the right of revolution.

So much for the origins of the doctrine up to the time of and including the Declaration of Independence.

Now let us turn and take a look at what happened in the 200 following years.

In the Constitutional Convention which met in Philadelphia in 1787, it is clear enough that the interest was not primarily in the doctrines set forth in the Declaration of Independence. What concerned those persons there assembled was the establishment of a representative government — an idea cognate to and congenial to the Declaration.

The Constitution itself uses the phrase "We, the people" in saying who it is that formed that Constitution. But, speaking generally, the problem which the Constitution dealt with was the disposition of power — its dispersal.

There were set up three branches of government, and their separation of powers was intended to limit the authority of government. The Constitution was in its nature federal, and thus there was the balance of the parts against the whole.

If you look at the Constitution itself, apart from amendments, what do you find that related to the Rights of Man? Oh, you will see a reference to habeas corpus, though a rather obscure one and difficult to interpret. You will also see — and this is quite interesting — measures with respect to the preservation of property, because contracts are to be protected against impairment.

And one would do well to remember, because it is often forgotten, that in the eyes of the framers of not merely the Constitution, but the Declaration of Independence, and, believe it or not, the French Declaration of Rights, the idea of property as a liberty was basic.

Speaking generally, the Declarations of Rights dealt with

civic and political questions, but when it came to property, there was an undeveloped awareness of a social or economic right.

The drafting of the Constitution in Philadelphia was, in some respects, unsatisfactory to the Colonists to whom it was to be submitted for ratification, and the chief complaint was the absence of a declaration or bill of rights. As we all know, the first ten amendments were adopted forthwith by the Congress and by the states in order that there might be specific recognition of some of the basic Rights of Man.

I need not remind you that in those provisions of the Bill of Rights, the first ten amendments to the Constitution, we have the guarantees of freedom of speech, freedom of press, freedom of religion, freedom of assembly, freedom of petition. We have specific provisions with respect to unlawful searches and seizures. We have guarantees of due process of law. We are reminded that when property is taken by the government, compensation must be paid therefore. We are assured jury trial in criminal cases, and also a grand jury.

But look at the total list. Is it not clear that what is being preserved are political and civil rights, not — speaking generally — economic, social, or cultural rights?

Now let's see what happened after the Constitution was adopted. If you look at the history of the next seventy years, you will see that although the Declaration of Independence was, of course, honored, reliance in political debate was rarely upon declarations of the Rights of Man. That was too dangerous a doctrine, for at once it suggested the problem of slavery, as was well recognized by William Lloyd Garrison and Wendell Phillips of this city, who frequently did refer to the doctrines of natural rights.

However, Daniel Webster, whose portrait hangs behind me, said precious little about the kind of rights which the Declara-

45

tion of Independence asserts. For him the issue was, in his own phrase, "Liberty and Union, Now and Forever." And in those days, Union was difficult to reconcile with Abolition.

It is no accident that a great lawyer of this Commonwealth — great in spite of the quotation I am going to give — Rufus Choate, wrote to another citizen of Massachusetts, Farley, that the Declaration of Independence was a set of "glittering generalities" — a phrase that was often quoted.

While Abraham Lincoln professed an admiration for the aspirations of the Declaration of Independence, the fact of the matter is that he, as the Gettysburg Address clearly shows, thought that representative government was the dominant quality of our American political contribution — not the Declaration of Rights in any form.

After the Civil War was over, the posture of the Declaration of Rights and the general situation with respect to natural rights underwent a very strange change.

As we all are aware, following the Civil War, there was an enormous industrial expansion in the United States. Corporations which had, of course, existed from the beginning, flourished, and there became a general increase in corporate activity — already noted in an earlier speech in this series. And efforts were made, both by the states and by the national government to pass legislation to regulate these enterprises.

And then strangely enough — or perhaps not so strangely — resourceful corporate lawyers saw that the Constitution and the Declaration of Rights had in them notions of freedom of contract — a liberty which was by these lawyers construed as being a liberty to avoid, or not be subject to, economic and social regulation. And in a series of cases, beginning as early as the *Slaughter House* cases, and going really as late as the Hoover administration and the Roosevelt administration, in arguments in the Supreme Court of the United States, the contention was made that social and economic regulation was invalid because it interfered with the natural rights declared.

Nowhere is this more convincingly set forth than in a Supreme Court opinion not otherwise very generally known — *Allgeyer* v. *Louisiana* — in which the total natural rights theory is used to demolish social and economic regulation.

Is it any wonder that Mr. Justice Holmes — to whom reference has already been made as *the great* lawyer of this Commonwealth — would have nothing to do with doctrines of natural law and thought them transparently absurd?

He knew what indeed every informed person knew: that use was being made of those doctrines primarily to prevent effective public control of private greed.

The tide changed; and without going through all of the factors or trying to estimate how much was due to theoretical challenge — how much was due to legal skill — how much was due to the effects of a great depression — how much was due to a national leadership — we emerged from the period I've just described, and no longer could we be regarded as a limited liability state, functioning under the doctrines of John Locke. Instead, we became, as it were, one of the welfare states of the world, and governmental power was regarded quite differently from the way it was regarded by the Founding Fathers.

As I tried to say at the outset, the Founding Fathers, being fearful of governmental power, sought to disperse that power through doctrines such as the separation of powers and through an emphasis on the federal character of our Constitution. But people in the twentieth century became aware that, at least in some hands, if not all hands, government might be used for the beneift of the people and could be regarded as an affirmative force helping them to realize their vision, and not merely a danger to be guarded against, and a kind of power to be feared, limited, and separated.

So we came into a period — the one in which we now live — in which liberty was not necessarily thought to be achieved by limiting government, but sometimes it was thought that liberty could be achieved by using government. An emphasis was placed upon equality as well as upon liberty.

At the outset, men like Lord Acton had said that equality was the enemy of liberty. But those who were less fortunate in their heritage and their finances than Lord Acton were not quite so clear that equality was the enemy of liberty. For without some degree of equality — not absolute equality, to be sure — how can liberty be? Without some economic and social assurance, who cares about freedom of speech? Who cares about freedom of assembly or of press? Who cares about all those intellectual methods of communication and enjoyment?

Are we not the prisoners, for the most part, of our own privilege? Is it not the affluent and the educated who care most about these liberties of communication and expression? For the poor and the disadvantaged, the first necessity is some degree of economic and social equality.

And so it is that the Rights of Man have begun to develop in a way which emphasizes equality as much as, and as complementary to, liberty. The ways this has been achieved have been in part through legislation — some by laws such as the National Labor Relations Act and the Social Security Act, to which some reference was made in the introduction; some by doctrines in part invented by the Supreme Court of the United States in connection with the interpretation of the 5th and 14th Amendments to the Constitution. The guarantee of "equal protection of the laws" read with historical accuracy deals with equality before the law; but as now read by the Supreme Court of the United States, it deals with economic and social equality. And one finds words like "entitlement," which to the initiated means a method of making sure that people who do not have tangible property have something akin to a property interest which is protected by the majesty of the law and which is used as a device to increase the scope of individual liberty.

Moreover, using that and other clauses of the Constitution, we have seen a recognition of racial equality, and of equality between the genders so that men and women are treated alike. And in other ways through imaginative judicial reasoning — in general, but not universally, as we are reminded in this community — approved by the people, there has been a totally new development of the Rights of Man.

Simultaneously, with a greater sensitivity mostly to the disadvantaged, there has been a development of the area of civil liberties. As recently as thirty years ago, when Professor Commager surveyed all the cases in the Supreme Court of the United States which dealt with civil liberties and civil rights, he was only able to emerge with a slim volume — listing less than a hundred cases.

Today, in every court, not least of all the one in which the mayor has an interest, there are cases presenting issues of civil liberties and civil rights.

Moreover, those who have the misfortune to be charged with crimes know to what extent the courts are today sensitive to the civil liberties and claims of defendants.

The press and the media have by now a degree of legal protection totally unknown when I was born. I do not exaggerate when I say that Mr. Justice Holmes, when he became a Justice of the Supreme Court of the United States in 1902, did not believe that freedom of the press was protected against infringement by any *state* law, and he thought that the degree of

49

protection available against an act of Congress was really almost as limited as Blackstone had thought.

The whole area is in ferment, and rights everywhere are acquiring a new status and a new power.

But now, so much for the two hundred years, and let us turn to the prospect.

If you have noted what I have been saying, you have been aware that one of the kinds of liberty and equality with which we have been recently concerned has been of special interest to groups — racial groups, other disadvantaged groups, groups who represent one sex, groups who represent economic and social pressures.

Now, there are those who deplore such pressure groups. How little they understand democracy! De Tocqueville, when he came in 1835 on an errand to study our penal institutions, returned to France to write the great classic, *Democracy in America*. And among the themes in that book, none is more important than his recognition of the role of voluntary associations and of groups.

One cannot effectively participate in a modern society except through a group. The Declaration of Rights in its origin is rather primitive. It treats Man as though he were a viable atom. But Man is indeed more molecular than atomic. It is in combination that Man is effective, and one cannot truly have participatory democracy, one cannot realize the promise inherent in decisions amplifying the "one man, one vote" approach of *Baker* v. *Carr,* unless one is prepared to recognize the power of groups.

There's nothing wrong with the phrase "Black Power." It's very perceptive. There's nothing wrong with the idea of Women's Liberation. It has its impact, let us not doubt it.

What we are to be concerned with in the future is not the destruction of those groups, it is the problem of their interrelation and their inner life.

The greatest man who lived in this community in the twentieth century, Alfred North Whitehead, in his most remarkable book, *Adventures of Ideas,* foresaw that it was the relationship between one group and another, and it was the internal structures of those groups, which would be the great concern of the future of public and legal development. We are merely on the threshold of understanding this, and, indeed, right here in this community, we are in the throes of difficulties created by a failure to understand.

No one could have more admiration for the decency, the conviction, and the courage of my fellow federal judge, Judge Garrity, than I have. He is faced with a problem in this city because we never have realized what we were doing with respect to claims of groups, and I do not mean of one, as distinguished from another, color, or one as distinguished from another ethnic origin. It is a total mistake to assume that men may be homogenized.

I noticed that the mayor called me a controversial character. I hope I am. To be controversial is to be nonconventional, to be independent, to recognize that "strife is the source of all things," as Heraclitus said. We must recognize that the tensions between groups are of the very essence of a vital society. It is through competition and conflict that men become creative and societies endure. And we must have the imagination and sympathy to recognize that.

If it be true that the problem of groups is one of those we see in prospect and indeed in present difficulties, there is another which deals with the individual perhaps more in the original sense of the Declaration of Human Rights.

Those who framed the Constitution were not consciously discriminatory. Very few people are. But did they realize their bias against women? Did they realize their bias against those groups which could not be classified as WASPs? Did they see that they in some sense thought that the future of

America was assimilationist? Was that a shortcoming of theirs?

For every human being, no matter what his background, is potentially an asset. His creative powers, whatever they may be, are a community resource as well as a matter of personal joy. And part of the task of our society is not to stop with liberty and with equality, but to remember that there is a great deal in the third of the allied aspects of democracy — fraternity.

It is only when we perceive that, for each individual, his stability and happiness will depend upon our recognizing, in Isaiah's words, that "the rock whence . . . [he is] hewn" is part of what we need for the building of our common structure, that we shall have really achieved democracy, and that we shall have recognized that here on earth as well as in heaven, "my Father's house has many mansions."

There is every reason that in this Commonwealth, we should take special pride that, by common consent, the best statement of a Declaration of Rights ever made was in the 1780 Declaration in our original Constitution and in our present Constitution — for that part remains unaltered. And let it serve as a reminder that the way that that Declaration begins is — and I quote — it is "a Declaration of the Rights of the *inhabitants* of the Commonwealth." For each person and for all persons, for them as individuals and for us as a group, may their rights forever be precious!

Questions and Discussion

Judge Wyzanski and his statement on "The Rights of Man" were given a standing ovation, and at the same moment a sheaf of questions were handed up from the floor. These ranged from the rights of women to the nationalization of the oil industry and the growing scope and power of government. From among them the judge chose for an extended answer one about the relative advantages and disadvantages of big government.

"Today it is plain," he began, "that the increase in technological complexity requires a vast amount of bureaucratic regulation. The numbers of persons and of their contacts have changed the problem of balancing liberty and quality. The mayor said earlier that this country had multiplied seventy times in population in the past 200 years. He might have referred to Brossard's Law, that as population increases arithmetically, contacts increase geometrically. Thus each of us has many more contacts than people had 200 years ago, and we require regulation.

"Nor is it necessarily true that increase in government is a bad thing. Mr. Justice Holmes is often quoted as saying, 'I love to pay taxes. It is the price of good government.' Now that is a rather optimistic view, but it is still true that it is the public which will create for most of us the schools, the museums, the cultural and social experiences that are the sources of a better life — the playgrounds, the parks, the vistas.

"The question we are answering did not come from someone living in poverty. He reflects, probably without knowing it, the bias that comes to all who enjoy prosperity and privilege. We do not realize how much public money must be spent if we really intend that each person fulfill his potential.

"Not everybody can pay for his children's schooling out of his own pocket. Not everybody out of his own pocket can have a garden in his backyard, or a place to go for vacations. Not everybody can buy books to educate himself. All these sources for the development of personality depend on our willingness to use public funds for the benefit of all and to recognize that each man and woman and child is not a means to our influence and affluence, but an end in himself."

DISCUSSION AT PARKMAN HOUSE

The evening discussion at the Parkman House [1] began by exploring the complex relations between liberty and equality. The judge acknowledged that people are obviously not equal in physical or intellectual endowment, or in the accidents of wealth, position, and culture.

"But equality and liberty should not be looked upon as absolutes. It is not merely a question of total liberty or total equality. There must be some accommodation between the two. And in some important ways this has been happening.

"One of our problems today is how far we can enforce minimal standards without unduly interfering with people's initiative, their individual differences, their variety, their unconventionality, and the original contributions they may make."

On this point Robert Bergenhein, publisher of the Boston *Herald American*, recalled that the judge had been hearing cases on fairness in civil service examinations for police candidates of different ethnic backgrounds, and the judge replied that the issue in these cases had been equality of opportunity. On tests, he pointed out, most people reflect their own racial, cultural, and educational biases. Thus in effect candidates are selected on how well they conform to the standards of the dominant cultural and ethnic group, the one that determines

1. In addition to Judge and Mrs. Wyzanski, the group included Kevin H. White, Mayor of Boston; Sandy Burton, Bureau Chief, Time, Inc.; Robert Bergenhein, publisher Boston *Herald American;* Abram T. Collier, Chairman, New England Mutual Life Insurance Company; Edith Angelis, chairperson, East Boston Recreation and Land Use Council; Evelyn Dubrow, Legislative Representative, International Ladies Garment Workers; Howard Johnson, President of the Corporation, Massachusetts Institute of Technology; Elma Lewis, Director, Elma Lewis School of Fine Arts; J. Anthony Lukas, reporter, *New York Times;* David L. Rosenbloom, Executive Assistant to the Mayor of Boston; Thomas Sampson, President of Arthur Anderson Company and Chairman of Boston 200; Dennis Shaul, former Commissioner of Commerce for the State of Ohio; Sam Bass Warner, Jr., Professor of History and Social Science, Boston University.

the content of the test. The result is a distorted reflection of equality of opportunity. One of the most difficult things for our society to recognize is that because we are a pluralist people a simple standard examination does not accurately show the potential of all our ethnic varieties.

"Genetically there is no very great difference between peoples. Most differences are largely effects of culture. Nurture counts more than nature in these differences. Every group can be graphed by an onion-shaped curve in which the tip is clearly outstanding. If we tested only the tips we would probably have a better sample of the potential capacity of our population than when we apply any kind of overall examination which ignores the differences.

"And yet great advances have been made in our time in other aspects of equality. I recall that in 1933 Sidney Hillman, then President of the Amalgamated Clothing Workers, came into my office in the Department of Labor one day, and showed me a worker's weekly paycheck — his compensation for a whole week's work — in the amount of two dollars! No one now thinks it desirable to have a totally open market for labor, a market which can let economic forces drive people to starvation. There is a general appreciation of the necessity for a minimum wage. I'm not now talking about what that wage should be, or how it should be fixed. But we do now agree that there should be a floor somewhere. This is a great advance in the area of equality.

"But there are three desirable social qualities to be fostered in a democracy, not just two — liberty, equality, *and fraternity*. Any stable society which purports to be democratic takes all these into account and recognizes that no one of them will flourish if the others are ignored."

The discussion was then brought back to the question of *property rights* and their importance to individuals in relation to the power of the state. Is not a state powerful enough to redistribute income also able to overturn traditional ideas about civil rights?

The judge responded at length to this question. "United States law crossed a dividing line without knowing it when in 1913 it adopted the 16th Amendment, establishing a federal income tax. It took us a long time to understand that we had moved into a society of redistributive justice. The moment a government takes a very large fraction of your income it is in one sense curtailing the interests of private property, acting in a way that would not have commanded the support of John Adams, Thomas Jefferson, or any of the Founding Fathers.

"Inequalities of fortune are socially justified to the extent that they reward talent, industry, and energy. But nobody can argue that vast differences in fortune reflect actual differences in capacity or contributions to the society. Now we have crossed this Rubicon, we are faced with making judgments about how far we ought to go. Few people anywhere in the United States argue for strict equality of income. Yet most would agree that there are certain kinds of property which ought to be public, not private. I will not try to specify what these should be. Different people would draw the line in different places; but lines *must* be drawn.

"The more troublesome aspect of this subject derives from the power of government to redistribute. When you give government the power to redistribute money, you vest in it an enormous capacity to act capriciously, arbitrarily, corruptly, along some particular line which either intentionally or unintentionally cuts off diversity, variety, experiment, creativity, growth, and all the things we deem most desirable in a democratic system. The original restraints which were thought adequate in the Constitution are no longer so. We are no longer a truly federal government; we are federal in form, but the national power has become supreme."

It was then asked what upper and lower income limits the

judge had in mind, and the group was reminded that in Cuba the allowed range, in terms of U.S. equivalents, was from $10,000 to $70,000. Some such range might provide a powerful philosophical argument for the pluralism of cultures and interests and give some practical basis on which to take action. The economist Milton Friedman would agree that if there were more money in the black community, for example, it would need less governmental protection and could speak better for itself.

The judge replied that he did not wish to answer an economic question as if it were a political one. Questions about quantity are economic, he said; political questions deal with shared values in the community, and that was what he wanted to talk about.

"What we are really dealing with is *the total nature of man in society*, and we begin with an error when we say this can be seen solely in terms of income, or capital, or other property. It is equally wrong to think that it can be seen purely in points of law. Unfortunately the statement of John Adams written into the Massachusetts constitution is in serious error. Adams said, and the constitution repeats: 'We live under a government of laws and not of men.' Now laws are an abstraction, and we are individuals. It is the nature of the social problem to see how individuals, acting individually and in groups, and collectively as a total, behave in their value structures and value arrangements. We live under a government of men. And each man and woman is responsible for the society in which we live.

"We have more and more tended to regard people in their roles as expert or professional, in their occupation or race, instead of looking at them as whole men. And we have neglected the importance which Plato recognized and all other serious thinkers have recognized — the development of the total man, the well-rounded man, as necessary to a healthy so-

57

ciety. What we require is education in the obvious. *Education* in what it is that makes a man. We have neglected education toward improved awareness of being a citizen."

THE RADIO AUDIENCE

The National Public Radio network broadcast "The Rights of Man" Sunday evening, April 20, 1975,[2] and the audience talked mainly about individual liberties. How could the rights of the individual be defended against such things as gun control? How much did the right to have a large family conflict with the need to control the size of the population? How could a citizen defend himself against government when it could seize his property for taxes without trial? One listener was worried that the individual is nearly powerless against the large corporation, labor union, political party, or other organization armed with money, skilled counsel, and all the rights of due process.

The judge replied that while he sympathized with this comment, we have increasingly regulated groups. Many must now register with a government agency, spend their money only in restricted ways, and report on how they spend it. They actually are restrained by the antitrust laws, and legislatures are working steadily to create an open society without abuse of power.

A related legal reform is legal aid for the poor, which increasingly in the past ten years has helped many who could not have afforded a lawyer. Today some 3000 lawyers, through neighborhood and other service centers, are provid-

2. Again Sander Vanocur served as moderator, and Judge Wyzanski was joined by panelists John Silber, President of Boston University, and Jerome J. Shestak, a Philadelphia attorney long active with the American Bar Association and other groups working for human rights. Questions were phoned in from all parts of the United States.

ing help against powerful interests on such matters as housing, welfare, equal employment opportunity, and consumer law. It has not yet come to the point where legal services are looked upon as a right in civil cases, though they are in criminal; but we are moving in that direction. Here was a clear case of new human rights in process of development.

Finally, audience and panel fruitfully discussed the question how far American ideas on the rights of man had spread throughout the world. Judge Wyzanski sketched our abortive role in the United Nations on questions of human rights. In 1966, he said, two different covenants were adopted by the Assembly of the United Nations, one relating to political and civil rights, the other to social, economic, and cultural rights. These conventions will come into force when a sufficient number of countries assent. The United States, far from assenting, has been a dog in the manger on this matter, although it was our representative, Eleanor Roosevelt, who chaired the original commission, and it was she who first wanted a declaration of essential human rights.

The State Department and the Congress have never shown much interest in making us in any way party to such an international covenant. We are apparently afraid that because of certain internal problems, we ourselves may be hailed before a tribunal. The British, the French, and others who are not our inferiors in democracy, have been willing to set up a committee in connection with this matter. There is now a commission on human rights, before which parties are free to arraign governments as democratic as that of the United Kingdom. It is we who are to blame for not having an effective international covenant, the judge concluded.

Panelist Shestak admitted that the United States could do more to champion human rights internationally but thought human rights were being violated by a multitude of other nations as well. In 1948 when the universal declaration of human rights was adopted, it was to be a kind of bill of rights for the world. It carried high hopes and much promise. Some twenty-seven years later the story around the world is still a sad one. South Africa pursues a vicious policy of apartheid, impervious to U.N. resolutions. Brazil and Chile torture prisoners. Uganda expels long-term residents. Syria and Iraq persecute the Jews. The Soviet Union represses dissidents and denies them the right to leave. France abuses Algerian workers. The world produces a litany of gross violations of human rights.

The U.N. has become so politicized that it does almost nothing about this issue. If a nongovernmental organization interested in human rights, such as the International League for the Rights of Man on Amnesty, comes before the U.N. Commission on Human Rights, it is not even allowed to name the offending nation!

In short, panel and audience agreed that the combined causes of liberty, equality, and fraternity have been advancing by an uncertain path, but that we have made progress and should not cease to struggle and to hope.

4

Home to Roost

HANNAH ARENDT

By the afternoon of May 20, when Professor Arendt gave her address on criminality in government, which she titled "Home to Roost," summer had come to Boston in earnest. Through some executive foresight the occasion had been scheduled for the air-conditioned New England Life Hall, a familiar meeting place in the Back Bay section of Boston's downtown. The decor of the hall and even the date on the cornerstone of the building in which it is located — 1940 — reflected one main focus of the speaker, the era of Roosevelt's Washington, Hitler's Berlin, and Stalin's Moscow.

The room filled early with an audience of young and old drawn to hear a lady and a scholar known as America's most thoughtful writer on the mechanisms of totalitarian horror. Now University Professor at the New School for Social Research in New York City, Ms. Arendt has had a varied career. Twice a refugee, once from her native Germany and then from France, she came to this country in 1941. Trained as a philosopher, she has been a successful book editor, has been active in Jewish cultural affairs, and has served on the faculties of a number of American universities. She first attracted national attention with her book on the holocaust, The Origins of Totalitarianism (1951).

A frail lady with an intellect afire, she spoke words of passion in a gentle voice. From the lectern she looked out at her audience with both challenge and appeal: a challenge to face the facts from one who has spent much of a lifetime trying to understand the horrors of the modern world; an appeal to view the world with the balanced perspective of one who has seen the best and the worst of it.

LADIES AND GENTLEMEN:

We have come here together to celebrate a birthday party, the two-hundredth birthday not of America but of the Republic of the United States, and I fear we could not have chosen a less appropriate moment. The crises of the Republic, of this form of government, and its institutions of liberty could be detected for decades, ever since what appears to us today as a mini-crisis was triggered by Joe McCarthy. A number of occurrences followed which testified to an increasing disarray in the very foundations of our political life: to be sure the episode itself was soon forgotten, but its consequence was the destruction of a reliable and devoted civil service body, something relatively new in this country, probably the most important achievement of the long Roosevelt administration. It was in the aftermath of this period that the "ugly American" appeared on the scene of *foreign* relations; he was then hardly noticeable in our domestic life, except in a growing inability to correct errors and repair damages.

Immediately thereafter a small number of thoughtful spectators began to have doubts whether our form of government would be able to withstand the onslaught of this century's inimical forces and survive the year 2000 — the first to utter such doubts publicly, if I remember rightly, was John Kennedy. But the general mood of the country remained cheerful and no one was prepared, not even after Watergate, for the recent cataclysm of events, tumbling over one another, cascading like a Niagara Falls of history whose sweeping force leaves everybody, spectators who try to reflect on it and actors who try to slow it down, equally numbed and paralyzed. The swiftness of this process is such that even to remember in some order "what happened when" demands a serious effort; indeed "anything that is four minutes old is as ancient as Egypt" (Russell Baker).

No doubt the cataclysm of events that numbs us is due to a large extent to a strange but in history by no means unknown coincidence of occurrences, each of which has a different meaning and a different cause. Our defeat in Vietnam — by no means a "peace with honor" but on the contrary an outright humiliating defeat, the helter-skelter evacuation by helicopter with its unforgettable scenes of a war of all against all, certainly the worst possible of the administration's four options to which we added gratuitously our last public-relations stunt, the baby airlift, the "rescue" of the only part of the South Vietnamese people who were entirely safe — the defeat by itself could hardly have resulted in so great a shock; it was a certainty for years, expected by many since the Tet offensive.

That "Vietnamization" would not work could have our prised nobody; it was a public-relations slogan to excuse the evacuation of American troops who, ridden by drugs, corruption, desertions, and plain rebellion, could no longer be left there. What came as a surprise was the way Thieu himself, without even consulting his protectors in Washington, managed to accelerate the disintegration of his government to such an extent that the victors were unable to fight and conquer; what they found, when they could make contact with an enemy who fled more rapidly than they could pursue him, was not an army in retreat but an unbelievable rout of a mob of soldiers and civilians on a rampage of gigantic proportions.

However, the point is that this disaster in Southeast Asia

63

occurred almost simultaneously with the ruin of the foreign policy of the United States — the disaster in Cyprus and possible loss of two former allies, Turkey and Greece, the coup in Portugal and its uncertain consequences, the debacle in the Middle East, the rise to prominence of the Arab states. It coincided in addition with our manifold domestic troubles: inflation, devaluation of currency, the plight of our cities, the climbing rate of unemployment and of crime. Add to this the aftermath of Watergate, which I think is by no means behind us, the trouble with NATO, the near bankruptcy of Italy and England, the conflict with India, and the uncertainties of détente, especially in view of the proliferation of nuclear arms, and compare it for a moment with our position at the end of the Second World War, and you will agree that among the many unprecedented events of this century the swift decline in power of the United States should be given due consideration. It, too, is almost unprecedented.

We may very well stand at one of those decisive turning points of history which separate whole eras from each other. For contemporaries entangled, as we are, in the inexorable demands of daily life, the dividing lines between eras may be hardly visible when they are crossed; only after people stumble over them do the lines grow into walls which irretrievably shut off the past.

At such moments in history when the writing on the wall becomes too frightening, most people flee to the reassurance of day-to-day life with its unchanging pressing demands. And this temptation today is all the stronger, since any long-range view of history, another favorite escape route, is not very encouraging either: the American institutions of liberty, founded two hundred years ago, have survived longer than any comparable glories in history. These highlights of man's historical record have rightfully become the paradigmatic models of our tradition of political thought; but we should not forget that, chronologically speaking, they were always exceptions. As such they survive splendidly in thought to illuminate the thinking and doing of men in darker times. No one knows the future, and all we can say with certainty at this rather solemn moment is: no matter how it will end, these two hundred years of Liberty with all its ups and downs have earned Herodotus' "due meed of glory."

However, the time for this long-range view and the glorification inherent in remembrance has not yet come, and the occasion quite naturally tempts us to recapture, as has been proposed, "the extraordinary quality of thought, speech and action" of the Founders. This, I am inclined to believe, might have been impossible under the best of circumstances because of the truly "extraordinary" quality of these men. It is precisely because people are aware of the fearful distance that separates us from our extraordinary beginnings that so many embark upon a search for the roots, the "deeper causes" of what happened. It is in the nature of roots and "deeper causes" that they are hidden by the appearances which they are supposed to have caused. They are not open to inspection and analysis but can be reached only by the uncertain way of interpretation and speculation. The content of such speculations is often far-fetched and almost always based on assumptions which are prior to an impartial examination of the factual record — there exists a plethora of *theories* about the "deeper" cause for the outbreak of the First or Second World War based not on the melancholy wisdom of hindsight but on the speculations grown into convictions about the nature and fate of capitalism or socialism, of the Industrial or post-Industrial Age, the role of science and technology, and so on. But such theories are even more severely limited by the implied demands of the audience to which they are addressed. They

65

must be *plausible*, that is, they must contain statements that most reasonable men at the particular time can accept; they cannot require an acceptance of the unbelievable.

I think that most people who have watched the frantic, panic-stricken end of the Vietnam war thought that what they saw on their television screens was "unbelievable," as indeed it was. It is this aspect of reality, which cannot be anticipated by either hope or fear, that we celebrate when Fortuna smiles and that we curse when misfortune strikes. All speculation about deeper causes returns from the shock of reality to what seems plausible and can be explained in terms of what reasonable men think is possible. Those who challenge these plausibilities, the bearers of bad tidings, who insist on "telling it as it is," have never been welcomed and often not been tolerated at all. If it is in the nature of appearances to hide "deeper" causes, it is in the nature of speculation about such hidden causes to hide and to make us forget the stark, naked brutality of facts, of things as they are.

This natural human tendency has grown to gigantic proportions during the last decade when our whole political scene was ruled by the habits and prescriptions of what is euphemistically called public relations, that is, by the "wisdom" of Madison Avenue. It is the wisdom of the functionaries of a consumer society who advertise its goods to a public, the larger part of which spends much more time in consuming its wares than it takes to produce them. Madison Avenue's function is to help distribute the merchandise, and its interest is focused less and less on the needs of the consumer and more and more on the need of the merchandise to be consumed in larger and larger quantities. If abundance and superabundance were the original goals of Marx's dream of a classless society in which the natural surplus of human labor — that is, the fact that labor stimulated by human needs always produces more than is necessary for the individual survival of the laborer and the survival of his family — then we live the reality of the socialist and communist dream, except that this dream has been realized beyond the wildest fantasies of its author through the advancement of technology whose provisional last stage is automation; the noble dream has changed into something closely resembling a nightmare.

Those who wish to speculate about the "deeper" cause underlying the factual change of an early producer society into a consumer society that could keep going only by changing into a huge economy of waste, would do well to turn to Lewis Mumford's recent reflections in *The New Yorker*. For it is indeed only too true that the "premise underlying this whole age," its capitalist as well as its socialist development, has been "the doctrine of Progress." "Progress," Mumford says, "was a tractor that laid its own roadbed and left no permanent imprint of its own tracks, nor did it move toward an imaginable and humanly desirable destination. 'The going is the goal,' " but not because there was an inherent beauty or meaningfulness in the "going." Rather to stop going, to stop wasting, to stop consuming more and more, quicker and quicker, to say at any given moment enough is enough would spell immediate doom. This progress, accompanied by the incessant noise of the advertisement agencies, went on at the expense of the world we live in, and of the objects with their built-in obsolescence, which we no longer use but abuse, misuse, and throw away. The recent sudden awakening to the threats to our environment is the first ray of hope in this development, although nobody, as far as I can see, has yet found a means to stop this runaway economy without causing a really major breakdown.

Much more decisive, however, than these social and economic consequences is the fact that Madison Avenue tactics under the name of public relations have been permitted to invade our political life. The Pentagon Papers not only showed

in detail "the picture of the world's greatest superpower killing or seriously injuring a thousand noncombatants a week,
while trying to pound a tiny backward nation into submission
on an issue whose merits are hotly disputed" — a picture
which in Robert McNamara's carefully measured words was
certainly "not a pretty one." The papers also proved beyond
doubt and in tedious repetition that this not very honorable
and not very rational enterprise was exclusively guided by the
needs of a superpower to create for itself an *image* which
would *convince* the world that it was indeed "the mightiest
power on earth."

The ultimate aim of this terribly destructive war, which
Johnson let loose in 1965, was neither power nor profit, not
even anything so real as influence in Asia to serve particular
tangible interests for the sake of which prestige, an appropriate image, was needed and purposefully used. This was not
imperialist politics with its urge to expand and annex. The
terrible truth to be gleaned from the story told in these papers
was that the only permanent goal had become the *image* itself,
which was debated in countless memoranda and "options,"
that is, in the "scenarios" and their "audiences," the very language borrowed from the theater. For the ultimate aim, all
"options" were but short-term interchangeable means, until
finally, when all signs pointed to defeat, this whole official
outfit strained its remarkable intellectual resources on finding
ways and means to avoid *admitting* defeat and to keep the
image of the "mightiest power on earth" intact. It was at this
moment, of course, that the administration was bound to clash
head-on with the press and find out that free and uncorrupt
correspondents are a greater threat to image-making than
foreign conspiracies or actual enemies of the United States.
This clash certainly was triggered by the simultaneous publication of the Pentagon Papers in the *New York Times* and the
Washington Post, probably the greatest journalistic scoop of the

century, but it was actually unavoidable so long as newspaper-men were willing to insist on their right to publish "all the news that's fit to print."

Image-making as global policy is indeed something new in the huge arsenal of human follies recorded in history, but lying as such is neither new nor necessarily foolish in politics. Lies have always been regarded as justifiable in emergencies, lies that concerned specific secrets, especially in military matters, which had to be shielded against the enemy. This was not lying on principle, it was the jealously guarded prerogative of a small number of men reserved for extraordinary circumstances, whereas image-making, the seemingly harmless lying of Madison Avenue, was permitted to proliferate throughout the ranks of all governmental services, military and civilian — the phony body counts of the "search and-destroy" missions, the doctored after-damage reports of the air force, the constant progress reports to Washington, in the case of Ambassador Martin continuing up to the moment when he boarded the helicopter to be evacuated. These lies hid no secrets from friend or enemy; nor were they intended to. They were meant to manipulate Congress and to persuade the people of the United States.

Lying as a way of life is also no novelty in politics, at least not in our century. It was quite successful in countries under the rule of total domination, where the lying was guided not by an image but by an ideology. Its success as we all know was overwhelming but depended on *terror*, not on hidden persuasion, and its result is far from encouraging: quite apart from all other considerations, to a large extent this lying on principle is the reason that Soviet Russia is still a kind of underdeveloped and underpopulated country.

In our context, the decisive aspect of this lying on principle is that it can work only through terror, that is, through the invasion of the political processes by sheer criminality. This is what happened in Germany and Russia on a gigantic scale during the thirties and forties; when the government of two great powers was in the hands of mass murderers. When the end came, with the defeat and suicide of Hitler and the sudden death of Stalin, a political kind of image-making was introduced in both countries, though in very different ways, to cover up the unbelievable record of the past. The Adenauer regime in Germany felt it had to cover up the fact that Hitler had not only been helped by some "war criminals" but supported by a majority of the German people, and Khrushchev in his famous speech on the Twentieth Party Congress pretended that it all had been the consequence of the unfortunate "personality cult." In both instances, this lying was what we today would call a coverup, and it was felt to be necessary to enable the people to return from a monstrous past that had left countless criminals in the country and to recover some kind of normality.

As far as Germany was concerned, the strategy was highly successful and the country actually recovered quickly, whereas in Russia the change was not back to anything we would call normal but a return to despotism; and here we should not forget that a change from total domination with its millions of entirely innocent victims to a tyrannical regime which persecutes only its opposition can perhaps best be understood as something which is normal in the framework of Russian history. Today the most serious consequence of the terrible disasters of the thirties and forties in Europe is that this form of criminality with its blood baths has remained the conscious or unconscious standard by which we measure what is permitted or prohibited in politics. Public opinion is dangerously inclined to condone not crime in the streets but all political transgressions short of murder.

Watergate signified the intrusion of criminality into the political processes of this country, but compared to what had already happened in this terrible century its manifestations — blatant lying, as in the Tonkin resolution, to manipulate Congress, a number of third-rate burglaries, the excessive lying to cover up the burglaries, the harassment of citizens through the Internal Revenue Service, the attempt to organize a Secret Service exclusively at the command of the executive — were so mild that it was always difficult to take them altogether seriously. This was especially true for spectators and commentators from abroad because none of them came from countries where a constitution is actually the basic law of the land, as it has been here for two hundred years. So certain transgressions which in this country are actually criminal are not felt in other countries to be crimes.

But even we who are citizens, and who as citizens have been in opposition to the administration at least since 1965, have our difficulties in this respect after the selective publication of the Nixon tapes. Reading them, we feel that we overestimated Nixon as well as the Nixon administration — though we certainly did not overestimate the disastrous results of our Asian adventure. Nixon's actions misled us because we suspected that we were confronted with a calculated assault on the basic law of the land, with an attempt to abolish the Constitution and the institutions of liberty. In retrospect it looks as though there existed no such grand schemes but "only" the firm resolve to do away with any *law*, constitutional or not, that stood in the way of shifting designs inspired by greed and vindictiveness rather than by the drive for power or any coherent political program. In other words, it is as though a bunch of con men, rather untalented Mafiosi, had succeeded in appropriating to themselves the government of "the mightiest power on earth." It is in line with such considerations that the credibility gap, which the administration tells us threatens our relations with foreign countries, who allegedly no longer trust our commitments, is actually threatening domestic rather than international affairs. Whatever the causes for the erosion of American power, the antics of the Nixon administration with its conviction that dirty tricks are all you need to be successful in any enterprise are hardly among them. All this, to be sure, is not very consoling, but it is still the case that Nixon's crimes were a far cry from that sort of criminality with which we were inclined to compare it. Still, there are a few parallels which, I think, may rightfully claim our attention.

There is first the very uncomfortable fact that there were quite a number of men around Nixon who did not belong to the inner circle of his cronies and were not hand-picked by him, but who nevertheless stuck with him, some to the bitter end, even though they knew enough about the "horror stories" in the White House to preclude their mere manipulation. It is true that he himself never trusted them, but how could *they* trust this man who had proved throughout a long and not very honorable public career that he could *not* be trusted? The same uncomfortable question could of course, and with more justification, be asked about the men who surrounded and helped Hitler and Stalin. Men with genuinely criminal instincts acting under compulsion are not frequent, and they are less common among politicians and statesmen for the simple reason that their particular business, the business in the public realm, demands publicity, and criminals as a rule have no great desire to go public. The trouble, I think, is less that power corrupts than that the *aura* of power, its glamorous trappings, more than power itself, *attracts;* for all those men we have known in this century to have abused power to a blatantly criminal extent were corrupt long before they attained power. What the helpers needed to become accomplices in criminal activities was permissiveness, the assurance that they would be above the law. We don't know anything solid about these matters; but all speculations about an inherent tension between power and character suffer from a tendency to equate indiscriminately born criminals with those who only rush to help once it has become clear to them that public opinion or "executive privilege" will protect them from being punished.

As far as the criminals themselves are concerned, the chief common weakness in their character seems to be the rather naive assumption that all people are actually like them, that their flawed character is part and parcel of the human condition stripped of hypocrisy and conventional clichés. Nixon's greatest mistake — aside from not burning the tapes in time — was to have misjudged the incorruptibility of the courts and the press.

The cascade of events in the last few weeks almost succeeded for a moment in tearing to shreds the tissue of lies created by the Nixon administration and the web of the image-makers that had preceded it. Events brought out the undisguised facts in their brutal force, tumbling out into a heap of rubble; for a moment, it looked as though all the chickens had come home to roost together. But for people who had lived for so long in the euphoric mood of "nothing succeeds like success," the logical consequence that "nothing fails like failure" was not easy to accept. And thus it was perhaps only natural that the first reaction of the Ford administration was to try a new image that could at least attenuate the failure, attenuate the admission of defeat.

Under the assumption that "the greatest power on earth" lacked the inner strength to live with defeat, and under the pretext that the country was threatened by a new isolationism, of which there were no signs, the administration embarked upon a policy of recriminations against Congress, and we were offered, like so many countries before us, the stab-in-

73

the-back legend, generally invented by generals who have lost a war and most cogently argued in our case by General William Westmoreland and General Maxwell Taylor.

President Ford himself has offered a broader view than these generals. Noticing that time under all circumstances has the peculiarity of marching *forward,* he admonished us repeatedly to do as time does, he warned us that to look backward could only lead to mutual recriminations — forgetting for the moment that he had refused to give unconditional amnesty, the time-honored means to heal the wounds of a divided nation. He told us to do what he had not done, namely, to forget the past and to open cheerfully a new chapter of history. Compared to the sophisticated ways in which for many years unpleasant facts were swept under the rug of imagery, this is a startling return to the oldest methods of mankind for getting rid of unpleasant realities — *oblivion.* No doubt, if it were successful, it would work better than all the images that tried to be substitutes for reality. Let us forget Vietnam, let us forget Watergate, let us forget the cover-up and the cover-up of the cover-up enforced by the premature presidential pardon for the chief actor in this affair, who even today refuses to admit any wrongdoing; *not amnesty but amnesia will heal all our wounds.*

One of the discoveries of totalitarian government was the method of digging giant holes in which to bury unwelcome facts and events, a huge enterprise which could be achieved only by killing millions of people who had been the actors in or the witnesses of the past. For the past was condemned to be forgotten as though it had never been. To be sure, nobody for a moment wanted to follow the merciless logic of these past rulers, especially since, as we now know, they did not succeed. In our case, not terror but persuasion enforced by pressure and the manipulation of public opinion is supposed to succeed where terror failed. Public opinion at first did not show itself to be very amenable to such attempts by the Executive; the first response to what happened was a rapidly increasing stream of articles and books about "Vietnam" and "Watergate," most of which were eager not so much to tell us the facts as to find out and teach us the lessons we are supposed to learn from our recent past, quoting again and again the old adage that "those who do not learn the lessons of history are condemned to repeat it."

Well, if history — as distinct from the historians who derive the most heterogeneous lessons from their interpretations of history — has any lessons to teach us, this Pythian oracle seems to me more cryptic and obscure than the notoriously unreliable prophecies of the Delphic Apollo. I rather believe with Faulkner, "The past is never dead, it is not even past," and this for the simple reason that the world we live in at any moment *is* the world of the past; it consists of the monuments and the relics of what has been done by men for better or worse; its facts are always what has *become* (as the Latin origin of the word: *fieri — factum est* suggests). In other words, it is quite true that the past *haunts* us; it is the past's function to haunt us who are present and wish to live in the world as it really is, that is, has *become* what it is now.

I said before that in the cataclysm of recent events it was as though "all the chickens had come home to roost," and I used this common expression because it indicates the boomerang effect, the unexpected ruinous backfiring of evil deeds on the doer, of which imperialist politicians of former generations were so afraid. Indeed anticipating this effect actually restrained them decisively from whatever they were doing in faraway lands to strange and foreign people. Let us not count our blessings, but in quick and certainly not exhaustive form mention some of the most obvious ruinous effects for which it would be wise to blame no scapegoats, foreign or domestic, but only ourselves. Let us start with the economy whose sudden turn from boom to depression nobody predicted, and which the latest events in New York City so sadly and ominously dramatized.

Let me first say the obvious: inflation and currency devaluation are inevitable after lost wars, and only our unwillingness to admit a disastrous defeat leads and misleads us into a futile search for "deeper causes." Only victory together with acquisition of new territories and reparations in a peace settlement, can make up for the entirely unproductive expenses of war. In the case of the war which we have lost, this would be impossible anyhow since we did not intend to expand, and even offered (though apparently never intended to pay) North Vietnam two and a half billion dollars for the reconstruction of the country. For those eager to "learn" from history, there is the trite lesson that even the extravagantly rich can go bankrupt. But there is, of course, more to the sudden crisis that has overcome us.

The Great Depression of the thirties, which spread from the United States to all of Europe, was in no country brought under control or followed by a normal recovery — the New Deal in America was no less impotent in this respect than the notoriously ineffective *Notverordnungen,* the emergency measures of the dying Weimar Republic. The Depression was ended only by sudden and politically necessitated changes to a war economy, first in Germany, where Hitler had liquidated the Depression and its unemployment by 1936, and then with the outbreak of the War, in the United States. This tremendously important fact was noticeable to everybody, but it was immediately covered up by a great number of complicated economic theories, so that public opinion remained unconcerned. Seymour Melman is, as far as I know, the only writer of any consequence to make this point repeatedly (see *American Capitalism in Decline,* which according to a critic in *The New York Times Book Review,* "presents enough data to float three books this size"), and his work remains entirely outside the mainstream of economic theory. But while this basic fact, very frightening in itself, was overlooked in nearly all public debates, it resulted almost immediately in the more or less commonly shared conviction that manufacturing "companies are in business not to produce goods but to provide jobs."

This maxim may have had its origin in the Pentagon, but it certainly has meanwhile spread all over the country. It is true that the war economy as the savior from unemployment and depression was followed by the large-scale use of the various inventions which we sum up under the label of automation, and which, as was dutifully pointed out fifteen or twenty years ago, should have meant a brutal loss of jobs. But the debate over automation and unemployment quickly disappeared for the simple reason that featherbedding and similar practices partly, but only partly, enforced by the great power of the unions, have seemed to take care of the problem. Today it is almost universally accepted that we must make cars to keep jobs, not to move people about.

It is no secret that the billions of dollars demanded by the Pentagon for the armaments industry are necessary not for "national security" but for keeping the economy from collapsing. At a time when war as a rational means of politics has become a kind of luxury justifiable only for small powers, arms trade and arms production have become the fastest growing business, and the United States is "easily the world's largest arms merchant." As Canada's Prime Minister Pierre Trudeau, when criticized recently for selling arms to the United States that were eventually used in Vietnam, sadly stated, it has all become a choice "between dirty hands and empty bellies."

Under these circumstances, it is entirely true that, as Melman states, "inefficiency [has been elevated] into a national purpose," and what has come home to roost in this particular case is the hectic and unfortunately highly successful policy of "solving" very real problems by clever gimmicks which are only successful enough to make the problems temporarily disappear.

Perhaps it is a sign of a reawakening sense for reality that the economic crisis, highlighted by the possible bankruptcy of the country's largest city, has done more to push Watergate into the background than all the various attempts of two administrations put together. What still persists, and still haunts us, is the astounding aftermath of Mr. Nixon's enforced resignation. Mr. Ford, an unelected President, appointed by Mr. Nixon himself because he was one of his strongest supporters in Congress, was greeted with wild enthusiasm. "In a few days, almost in a few hours, Gerald Ford dispelled the miasma that hung so long over the White House; and the sun, so to speak, started shining in Washington again," said Arthur Schlesinger, certainly one of the last among the intellectuals one would have expected to nurture secret longings for the man on horseback. That was indeed how a great many Americans instinctively reacted. Mr. Schlesinger may have changed his mind after Ford's premature pardon, but what then happened showed how well attuned he had been to the mood of the country in his hasty evaluation. Mr. Nixon had to resign because he was sure to be indicted for the cover-up of Watergate; a normal reaction of those concerned with the "horror stories" in the White House would have been to follow up by asking who actually instigated this affair which then had to be covered up. But so far as I know this question was asked and seriously pursued by one lone article, by Mary McCarthy in *The New York Review of Books*. Those who had already been indicted and convicted for their roles in the cover-up were overwhelmed with very high offers from publishers, the press and television, and the campuses to tell their story. No one doubts that all these stories will be self-serving, most of all the story Nixon himself plans to publish, for which his agent thinks he can easily get a $2 million advance. These offers, I am sorry to say, are by no means politically motivated; they reflect the market and its demand for "positive images" — that is, its quest for more lies and fabrications, this time to justify the cover-up and to rehabilitate the criminals.

What comes home to roost now is this long education in imagery; which seems no less habit-forming than drugs. Nothing in my opinion told us more about this addiction than the public reaction, on the street, as well as in Congress, to our "victory" in Cambodia, in the opinion of many "just what the doctor ordered" (Sulzberger) to heal the wounds of the Vietnam defeat. Indeed, " ' 'Twas a famous victory!' " as James Reston aptly quoted in the *New York Times;* and let us hope that this was finally the nadir of the erosion of power in this country, the nadir of self-confidence when victory over one of the tiniest and most helpless countries could cheer the inhabitants of what only a few decades ago really was the "mightiest power on earth."

Ladies and Gentlemen, while we now slowly emerge from under the rubble of the events of the last few years, let us not forget these years of aberration lest we become wholly unworthy of the glorious beginnings two hundred years ago. When the facts come home to roost, let us try at least to make them welcome. Let us try not to escape into some utopias — images, theories, or sheer follies. It was the greatness of this Republic to give due account for the sake of freedom to the best in men and to the worst.

Questions and Discussion

Professor Arendt had argued that the dishonesty in American government that began with Senator McCarthy in the 1950s has now brought our world crashing about our ears, with the forced resignation of a President, the debacle in Vietnam, inflation, depression, the collapse of our foreign policy, and the crumbling of our image as the most powerful nation in the world. All our chickens had come home to roost.

From her three sets of respondents, in the hall, at the Parkman House,[1] and on radio,[2] Ms. Arendt's address stimulated questions and discussion over a wide range of topics, on and beyond her central argument. The most rewarding of these topics were the Founding Fathers and the Constitution, the presidency, the federal bureaucracy, its development and possible decline, the Supreme Court and the judiciary, totalitarianism, the helplessness of the modern voter, and accountability in government.

THE FOUNDING FATHERS AND THE CONSTITUTION

One group saw such recent events as Watergate and the debacle in Vietnam and Southeast Asia as a constitutional

1. Members of the Parkman House Seminar, May 20, 1975: Hannah Arendt, University Professor. New School for Social Research, New York City; David Brudnoy, commentator, *Channel 7 TV*; Alan Dershowitz, Professor of Constitutional Law, Harvard Law School; Howard W. Johnson, Chairman of the Corporation, Massachusetts Institute of Technology; George G. Joseph, Vice-President, Marketing, New England Mutual Life Insurance Company; Katherine Kane, Director, Boston 200; Walter Littlefield, Professor of Speech, Emerson College; Art Naperstek, Director of Policy Planning and Program Development, National Center for Urban Ethnic Affairs, Washington, D.C.; Nan Ottenbacher, President, Brighton Historical Society; Nan Robinson, Vice President for Planning, University of Massachusetts, Boston; David L. Rosenbloom, Executive Assistant to the Mayor of Boston; Henry F. Thoma, editor, Houghton Mifflin Company; Sam Bass Warner, Jr., Professor of History and Social Science, Boston University; and Tom Wicker, editorial writer, the *New York Times*.

2. Ms. Arendt's address was broadcast over National Public Radio the evening of Sunday, May 2, 1975. The moderator was Sander Vanocur, in Washington, D.C., and panelists were William B. Harvey, Professor of Law and Political Science at Boston University; Lee Ospitz, political writer and former president of the Ripon Society; and Joan Claybrook, director of the Congress Watch Project of Organization Public Citizen.

crisis and asked whether it would prove to be a passing aberration or would bring permanent change in U.S. politics. Ms. Arendt's view was that the Constitution would weather the storm. She saw the people who came together in Philadelphia at the Constitutional Convention in 1787 as a group whose like had not been assembled before. Neither idealists nor cynics, they pooled a remarkable knowledge of human nature and saw the enigmatic creature man as capable of both the best and the worst behavior. They saw themselves as engaged in an experiment, and the institutions of liberty they set up were meant to create conditions in which the worst would be restrained and the best could find expression. Yet they themselves committed grave sins. Some of them were slaveholders, and slavery in America was worse than any slavery known in antiquity

But the essential fact is that we have a constitution, and that it can be amended. Those of us who have not lived in less settled nations cannot appreciate what it means to have a basic law which has lasted, with interruptions and amendments to be sure, for two hundred years. We can speak of our Constitution in a way which is entirely different from that of a German, an Italian, or even an Englishman. We can speak of crimes against the Constitution. We have a basic law to guide us. That is the extraordinary achievement of the Founding Fathers. Few Americans are used to thinking of theirs as the oldest stable written constitution in existence. But it is, and that is its glory.

CHANGE IN THE PRESIDENCY

But why had the constitutional provisions which had preserved the Republic for two hundred years now suddenly failed, especially in the loss of restraints on the presidency? In part, because of original provisions in the Constitution. The Federalists feared that Congress would be the source of tyranny, that coalitions of regional and economic interests would band together in Congress to suspend the liberties of the citizens, as in fact they did against the Abolitionists before the Civil War and against Socialists and Communists after World Wars I and II. According to the expectations of the Founders, the presidency was a lesser threat, since any one man would hold that office for a short time only, and he would always be under the jealous supervision of Congress.

A chief cause of change was the increasing isolation of the President, which has taken place perhaps since the years of the Truman administration. As the nation has grown from a population of two million to two hundred million, the executive branch has grown with it, until the President is surrounded by such a battery of aides and secretaries and assistants that he has little or no direct contact with the people. Instead of running the country, he runs only the government, and even that to a limited degree, since the executive branch has become the largest single employer in the nation!

"But is the President then the master or the prisoner of the bureaucracy?" asked Tom Wicker of the *New York Times*. For example, he said, it was understood in the field in Vietnam that President Johnson wanted to hear only certain things. Perhaps therefore he was told only what he wanted to hear, and so became the victim of false reports.

No one can be more easily manipulated than the President; he is the ideal victim. He sits in the White House hearing nothing he does not want to hear. It is this isolation that makes the Imperial Presidency so dangerous.

THE BUREAUCRACY OR CIVIL SERVICE

For these and other reasons it is easy to see that a competent and independent bureaucracy or civil service is essential to the survival of our democracy. It is the people who are nearly independent who keep politics within the bounds of legality. We depend upon people of talent and energy, and reasonable independence, going into the civil service and keeping the government running properly.

The case of Robert McNamara, when he was Secretary of Defense, is an interesting example of the strengths and weaknesses of bureaucracy in recent years. It was he who encouraged the publication of the Pentagon Papers. But he did not feel that he could publicly acknowledge his responsibility for them or vouch for their accuracy, though they are superbly reliable. Imagine the boost it would have given to the Civil Service if he had asserted his independence over the incident and resigned his office.

It is probable that the quality of the federal civil service has improved in recent decades. During the great depression of the 1930s people of unusual talent were drawn into public service because of unemployment elsewhere and because of President Roosevelt's policy of employing experts who were not professional politicians. Opinions varied on whether the quality of civil servants has declined more recently, and some felt that Senator Joseph McCarthy's wholesale attack on what he called Communists in government drove many good men out. The civil service as such has never challenged or defied a President, nor does it need to challenge in order to defy. In Professor Arendt's words, "They don't have to be aggressive. They need only, like the Supreme Court, not to be 'yes men.' "

THE SUPREME COURT AND THE JUDICIARY

The great mass of the government bureaucracy is part of the executive branch. But it was Professor Arendt's view that what really saved us in the Nixon crisis was "the old men" of the Supreme Court, and the powerful sense of tradition they espouse, whether they come from the North or the South. It was a striking fact that the very men whom Nixon appointed to the Court voted against him on the crucial issue of executive privilege and the right to withhold the famous tapes from general knowledge. This case seemed to prove that the tradition of the Court is so strong that regardless of their politics, their background, and their personal affiliations, once men become justices of the Supreme Court they become genuinely impartial. The Court is in this a unique institution among modern states.

The view of an elevated judiciary, sustained by powerful traditions, and executed by old men of great probity, did not go unchallenged. Some saw the day-to-day performance of the judicial system as far from perfect, rarely impartial, and sometimes corrupt. A strong social hypocrisy was seen to motivate the three- to five-year sentences common for purse snatching in contrast to the light sentences given to white-collar criminals such as the Watergate offenders. Moreover the huge advances offered the latter by publishers for their memoirs argued a topsy-turvy world of false values and a preoccupation not with facts but with appearances.

IMAGES, AMERICAN AND EUROPEAN

The sense that we live in a world of public images carried the discussion beyond the constitutional crisis. Were there historical processes at work in the image-making of recent

American Presidents akin to those that shaped the propaganda of Hitler, Mussolini, and Stalin? The best answer to that question was that while we may be crossing one of the dividing lines of history, the present moment in this country is quite different from the times of Hitler and Stalin. In their countries it was a question of life and death to speak as you thought. You could not tell even your wife what you actually felt, for fear that she might accidentally reveal something which would destroy you. The essence of the power of Hitler and Stalin was a society atomized by terror, so that every person lived in the middle of an empty space, solitary, alone, and vulnerable. This vulnerability is the precondition to manipulation.

In the United States, individuals and groups still trust each other, even when our opinions are very different. The struggles of the students of the sixties are hard to explain, but seem more the products of voluntary association than of isolation. Even in the McCarthy years, when trust had declined in America, Hollywood was one of the few places where there was mutual denunciation and a loss of confidence like that which always occurs in a totalitarian regime.

The damage done here by images was of a different order. One of the most harmful of the self-delusions we live by is that of the United States as "the greatest power on earth." This concept has spawned dozens of other heroic but harmful images, about our technical competence and our practical wisdom as well as our military prowess and our enlightened leadership. No doubt the idea of the Imperial Presidency was another such harmful image, a style far removed from republican modesty or the judicial traditionalism of the Supreme Court.

VIETNAM AND WATERGATE

While constitutional and theoretical questions took up a good deal of the discussion, there was also a deep concern with the immediate, the Vietnam war and the spying and fraud of the Nixon administration. There was real question whether the American public had yet learned the lessons of Vietnam and understood why we had gone there in the first place. Urged on by President Ford, people were too willing to forget about it, and the media flood the nation with so many events each day that they contribute to the forgetfulness. These speculations led to one center of hurt and confusion, the indifference of the American public to the longest and costliest war we have ever fought and its impact on those who fought and those who believed that an anti-Communist majority in South Vietnam was in the end left to its fate. There were those who felt that we broke the morale of this group by failing to provide them with promised ammunition, arms, equipment, and money. But by far the larger number of respondents had come to believe that we were wrong to have gotten into the war and well off to get out of it, even the way we did.

On Watergate, while President Ford was eager to distract the public and get them to think about some happier future, the general opinion was one of satisfaction that the traditional machinery of the United States government had finally worked after all, though it was cumbersome and slow. Yet for all the relief at the outcome, the responses revealed a nation still deeply divided, hurt, frustrated, and uncertain. Most of the discussants had fused memories of these two great complexes of events. It was pointed out that in both the presidential campaigns of 1968 and 1972 the image overrode the reality. In the first the winning party asserted that it had an undisclosed plan for ending the war in Vietnam, and in the second it made a plea not to interrupt pending negotiations to end the war. In both, the big lie and the false image strongly affected the public's choices. For whatever comfort there might be in the point, it was noted that the American public had become "wonderfully sophisticated" and that politicians would in future have to think twice before they tried things everyone had got away with in the past. We should be happy, it was concluded, with the outcome of Watergate.

A MOOD OF FRUSTRATION

Watergate and the Vietnam war flushed out a variety of fears and worries, and for many respondents the dominant mood was one of anger and frustration. One saw a Spenglerian clash between the two titans, Russia and the United States. Another saw an America of diminished power playing second fiddle to an expanding China. One lady in the radio audience who had contributed a comment on an earlier address in the series phoned in again to say that she felt powerless and disenfranchised, and feared that many shared her feelings. She saw the nation in ruin, the elderly starving, the youth without future, the blacks in despair, the American Indians in revolt. Those without power have no place to look for protection; law and order shelter only government and economic institutions. For twenty years we have been deceived by the media and spied on by the FBI and the CIA, and during the Nixon administration by the Secret Service. Another saw the excesses of the Nixon administration as a defense of beleaguered private corporate enterprise. Still another felt that the failure of the press fully to expose the main actors in the Bay of Pigs operation during the Kennedy administration made deception by later Presidents mushroom. All were embarrassed at the extravagant rejoicing over the recapture of the merchant ship *Mayaguez*.

ACCOUNTABILITY

One thing that frustrates many citizens is the sense that they have no way to hold government decision-makers accountable. There ought to be a kind of lawsuit which citizens could file against civil servants who fail to carry out their responsibilities. Unfortunately the Supreme Court has just made the nearest thing to this kind of lawsuit, the class action suit, virtually impossible: another example of how the citizen's voice in government is taken away from him.

In short the mood of the discussion and the response to Professor Arendt's challenge to face the facts revealed a nation that had yet to heal the wounds of recent events, one that did not reflect the optimism of an easier day, that we could simply "turn the rascals out." No one dared hope that a change in leaders or political parties would erase or even counter the experience of Vietnam and Watergate.

Practical remedies for weakness in governmental procedures or in the corporate society likewise seemed insufficient answers to a mood in which all seemed to agree that major events had indeed occurred, perhaps even that Professor Arendt's "line" between one historical epoch and another had indeed been crossed. We had survived as a nation and had preserved the political forms which we had lived by for two hundred years. But the future seemed gravely in doubt. In the general mood of hurt, frustration, and confusion, it seemed beyond the willingness of most to contemplate.

5

The Compact with the People

PETER W. RODINO, JR.

*When Congressman Rodino came to Boston to deliver his Bicenten-
nial Forums lecture on June 16, 1975, people jammed New England
Life Hall to see and hear the David who had slain the presidential
Goliath. His announced title, "The Constitutional Power of Impeachment," led his audience to expect an insider's revelations
about the path taken to force the resignation of President Nixon.
But the Congressman did not go into the expected details; he
wanted instead to reassure his listeners that the experience had
confirmed the soundness of our inherited form of government, and
he wanted to lead them toward consideration of the tasks the nation faces in the future.*

*A representative from Newark, New Jersey, since 1948 and now
a senior member of the House, Mr. Rodino has long responded to
major public needs. He wrote numerous reports on civil rights
from 1957 on and served as floor manager for the breakthrough
1964 Civil Rights Bill. In 1965 he radically altered the immigration
laws, ending the prejudicial national origins quotas that had held
one people more worthy of entry than another. He was sponsor of
the Omnibus Crime Control and Safe Streets Act of 1968, which
marked the entry of the federal government into assistance to local*

89

law enforcement. And his chairmanship of the Judiciary Committee made the question of impeachment his primary responsibility when it arose in 1974.

ON MAY 12, 1376, Peter de la Mare, a country knight from Hereford and the newly chosen speaker of the House of Commons, stepped to the bar of the high court of Parliament and demanded in the name of the Commons the removal of the King's chamberlain for malfeasance in office.

Before it was through, the "good Parliament" had impeached and removed most of the court clique which ruled England in the name of the feeble and senile Edward III, including the King's powerful but hated mistress, Alice Perrers.

This was history's first recorded use of the device of impeachment to curb intolerable excess in the executive. As such, it was the lineal ancestor of Article II, Section 4, of our Constitution and of the proceeding by which Richard Nixon was forced to resign as President of the United States almost six hundred years later.

It was not, however, the first attempt of the English people to deal with misuse of the royal prerogative through the forms of the law.

Edward's own father had been deposed in 1327 as a result of the united opposition of the church and the barons to the excesses of his court and his inability to lead the nation in a time of almost constant threat of war.

And Edward's successor, his grandson Richard II, was forced to abdicate in 1399 when the entire nation rejected his ruthless attempts to destroy all who stood in the way of his quest for absolute power. In both instances the forms of law were very important, and Parliament, a relatively new institution, was heavily involved.

The participants in these extraordinary fourteenth-century

events groped for the proper formalities in which to cloak truly revolutionary actions. But in their fumbling for legalisms, their unswerving preference for collective legitimacy over the naked dagger or the cup of poison, can be seen the genius of the Anglo-American system of government.

The British in the fourteenth century had already grasped the point that any worthy concept of sovereignty was inevitably broader than a mere personal possession of the King. It had to be a trust, one held in those days it is true by hereditary right, but a trust nonetheless. As a trust, it could be abused; and in the event of intolerable abuse, the beneficiaries of that trust were entitled to an accounting and, if ultimately necessary, to the removal of the trustee.

Thus by 1649 the nation was impervious to the logic of Charles I's argument that as the sovereign he was inherently incapable of treason. He was convicted and beheaded as a traitor to his people.

This fundamental notion of limited sovereignty as a trust was implicit in the great charter, the Magna Carta, wrung from an unwilling and tyrannical King John at Runnymede in 1215 and renewed, sometimes grudgingly, by each of his successors. John was forced to admit that he, like his subjects, was ultimately subordinate to God and the law. Even he could not "sell justice" or deprive any man of life or limb except *"per legem terrae,"* by the law of the land.

This deep and abiding concern with process, this commitment to continuity and legitimacy, shaped the American Revolution, and it pervades the great social compact which emerged from that revolution. It is manifested both in the specific, limited grants of power to the federal government and in the careful erection of procedural barriers around the liberties of the individual.

Thus the heart of the Constitution, the Bill of Rights, is concerned exclusively with process. It secures to people, not a forty-hour work week or a car in every garage, but the right to be "free in their persons, houses, papers and effects from unreasonable searches and seizures," the right not to be compelled to incriminate themselves, the right to "due process of law" before the government can take their lives, their liberty or their property, the right to speak freely and to petition their government for redress of grievances.

Our Constitution is the product of a passionate faith that if the procedures are fair, the access of ideas to government unblocked and the mechanisms of adjustment and restraint adequately articulated, the fleeting and changing substance of government policy will most often serve the public interest.

In examining the state of our compact on the two-hundredth anniversary of its birth, we must ask whether that faith has been justified. And we must inquire at two levels. First, how well have the mechanisms of the Constitution worked? And second, is this concept of government adequate for the last quarter of the twentieth century and for the years beyond?

On the first level, the success of the recent impeachment proceeding was but one more demonstration of the delicacy and the durability of the machinery.

No American who had been through the Revolution was prepared to create an executive which could not be called strictly to account by the people for abuse of its powers. By emulating the English model of impeachment and placing the power of accusation in the House of Representatives, the writers of the Constitution ensured broad public approval of any attempt to remove the President. By requiring a trial of specific charges in the more remote and secure realm of the Senate and a two-thirds vote to convict, they sought to ensure fair and dispassionate consideration of the President's guilt or innocence.

The procedure is brilliantly designed. It is sufficiently cumbersome and requires a broad enough consensus under conditions of solemnity and reflection that it is unlikely (the example of Andrew Johnson notwithstanding) to be invoked except in the kind of extraordinary circumstances for which it was intended. Yet its very existence is a powerful deterrent to executive misconduct, and its workability in the event of real presidential abuse is now unquestionable.

Impeachment is but one of the interlocking and overlapping devices by which our three separate branches of government are given sufficient powers to function in the public interest, yet restrained from the ultimate destruction of the system. We call these devices "checks and balances."

I think it is clear that this system has generally worked quite well for almost two centuries. Throughout our history, whenever one branch of government has overstepped its Constitutional bounds, the levers of adjustment have been applied, or else the mere threat of their application has permitted the system to right itself.

Impeachment has sometimes played a role. In the very early days of the Republic, Justice Samuel Chase embodied the zeal of certain Federalist elements for prosecution of their political enemies under the infamous Alien and Sedition Acts. His vitriolic grand jury charges and his blatant political activity while occupying the Supreme Court bench aroused the wrath of the Jeffersonians, who captured the White House and the Congress in 1800.

Chase was impeached by the House, but acquitted by the Senate. The acquittal was fortunate, for a conviction would have established a precedent for political harassment of the judiciary. But equally important, the judges were impressed with the need to stay above partisan politics and have been considerably more circumspect in their behavior ever since.

Instances could be multiplied. Frustrated by the obstructionism of the Supreme Court, which blocked all attempts at vitally needed reform legislation in the 1920s and 1930s, President Roosevelt sought to pack the court in 1937 with additional justices of his own persuasion. He needed, however, the consent of the Congress, which in its wisdom declined to enact the necessary legislation. Once again, though, the serious threat of action was enough. Chief Justice Hughes began voting with the "liberal" bloc on the Court to create a new majority to uphold federal and state legislation protecting the economic interests of the people.

Faced with the new realities of a nuclear world, Presidents in our time have asserted more and more the power to make war in the nation's name without the intervention of Congress. The country, weary of involvement in Vietnam, skeptical of the premises of our foreign policy and unwilling to entrust absolute war-making powers to Presidents, rightly demanded public disclosure, debate, and approval. The Congress responded by passing the War Powers Act, which restored the original Constitutional balance.

Our system of overlapping powers has not merely served in a negative way to block attempts by one branch of the government to usurp the powers of another. It has also allowed one branch of government to take the lead when the others failed to accept their responsibities.

When Congress and the President were unable or unwilling in the years after World War II to take meaningful steps to end the pervasive racial injustice in this country, the Supreme Court showed the way with Constitutional decisions which restored the original impetus toward equality of the post–Civil War amendments.

And when long-standing malapportionment had left most of our legislatures in a state of utter paralysis, where dominant rural interests frustrated every attempt of the more numerous urban populations to deal with the urgent problems of the cities, the Court once again stepped in and ordered reapportionment in the name of equal protection of the laws.

The results have been dramatic. The civil rights revolution, begun by *Brown* v. *Board of Education,* gradually gathered steam through the fifties and sixties, until Congress enacted the Civil Rights Act of 1964 and the Voting Rights Act of 1965. The latter, together with the reapportionment mandated by the Court since 1962, has fostered a true revolution in attitudes and responsiveness at all levels of government.

The change was given poignant expression earlier this month, when one white congressman from the Deep South after another came forward in the House of Representatives to speak and to vote for the extension of the Voting Rights Act.

The system of checks and balances also served as a restraint upon the "tyranny of the majority." In a decade of rising hysteria about crime and strident calls for harsher treatment of persons accused of criminal activity, the Supreme Court has stood guard over the precious liberties and procedural guarantees of the Bill of Rights. Likewise, in the days of the cold war, the Court time and again checked the overzealousness of the Congress and others with decisions protecting the First Amendment rights of free speech and the press.

I recite these examples, not to divert our attention from the very real problems we face, but by way of suggesting that at the first level of our inquiry, the system has functioned satisfactorily.

We saw this most recently in the manner in which we called the most powerful man on earth to account for his public trust. The reliability of the Constitutional process has been tested successfully under conditions of maximum stress. My point, however, is that despite its flaws and its sluggishness, and despite the discord and the disjointed movement which are inherent in any popular form of government, "the system" has been working very well for many years. A nation which in thirty years has helped rebuild much of the world after a devastating war, given so many billions of dollars of its treasury

95

to poorer nations, dramatically raised the standard of living of its own people, ended legalized racism and made genuine progress toward bringing racial minorities into the mainstream of its economy and its politics, put an end by sheer popular demand to its leaders' prosecution of a hopeless and wrongly conceived war, and preserved the liberties of its people from the abuses of its highest elected official has more than a little of which to be proud.

Pride in the glories of the past, however, cannot keep at bay the harsh realities of the present, and the second question is much harder. Can a system predicated upon an imperative of procedural fairness adequately serve the interests of this nation in a time of impending collision between the needs of the world's fast-growing population and the shrinking resources of the earth?

We must ask the question, I submit, because the problems of today are unique in our history. They are problems essentially of the allocation of resources, but this ever-present question is intensified in our times by rising population, rising expectations, and impending shortages.

At the same time we are learning firsthand of some of the shortcomings of a free-market economy in a modern world and of the traumatic social side effects of rapidly advancing technology.

We are left with a series of contradictions and dilemmas.

The world's supplies of petroleum are limited. We are increasingly dependent, as domestic reserves are depleted, upon foreign oil. This dependence on foreign oil plays havoc with our international posture and threatens the stability of our domestic economy. Yet we find ourselves unable to throw off a depression without encouraging people to build and buy more cars. If there is one thing we clearly do not need today, it is more cars to consume more gasoline and increase our need for foreign oil. Yet we are reduced, as one of your earlier speakers put it, to building more cars, not to transport people, but to create jobs.

The technology of destruction created in the last forty years is unlike anything ever before dreamed of by man in his worst nightmares. We have lost count of the number of times that the United States and the Soviet Union possess the power to annihilate the world's population. At the same time, we have entered an era of détente with our principal adversaries of the last thirty years.

Relaxation of international tensions and our real desires for peace are frustrated, however, by the constraints of our economy, which has remained essentially on a wartime footing since World War II. Thus, for example, in the great debate two weeks ago over the future of military procurement in the post-Vietnam era, we heard our senators sadly admit that armaments programs could not be cut because it would cost jobs, that we must continue to make weapons, not for legitimate defense purposes, but to employ people. And so, we go on arming ourselves beyond any reasonable necessity, diverting heavy capital investment from peaceful purposes, and exporting arms to our friends in other countries to use against each other.

We have spent many billions of dollars in the last thirty years on education and on a genuine and determined effort to give our citizens a fair economic opportunity. Yet a large portion of our population remains economically helpless and dependent on the state. Even those who have received the best education we have to offer frequently find themselves unable to fit into a hostile economic environment.

At a time of rapidly rising expectations, and rising educational levels, our technology has rendered human labor perhaps our most expensive and expendable commodity. The phrase "labor-intensive" in our economy is synonymous with unprofitable. At all levels, from elevator operators to file

97

clerks to accountants to researchers to executives, people are replaced more cheaply with machines. And despite increasing economic regulation of the private sector, those who have jobs find the gains they have made endangered by runaway inflation.

At the other end of the economic spectrum we have a significant segment of our society almost entirely unaffected by the depression, and efforts to promote constructive changes are opposed by powerful entrenched interests. Yet even here record and near-record corporate profits mask a difficult and potentially dangerous situation, as inflation and adverse international developments weaken our ability to form and attract vital investment capital.

The problems are not confined to the domestic scene. The gap between rich and poor nations continues to grow. We have no planning for the allocation of diminished supplies of minerals and other raw materials. The world's population is increasing at a positively alarming rate, outstripping our food supply and distribution systems. Yet we continue to pay people not to produce food, and our farmers are squeezed while all of us pay more to eat.

Where do we come out? It is not my purpose in this forum to propose solutions to the problems I have outlined. I do not pretend to have answers. And such answers as we will find will not come easy, nor offer easy solutions. What I do want to say, however, is that I believe that these problems can best be solved within the framework of our present governmental institutions.

One of the standard axioms of American political theory has been, "That government governs best which governs least." Sadly, I think we can no longer ascribe to this view. The responsibilities of government in today's world are too immense. With a world population doubling in less than thirty years, with millions of people hungry, with vital commodities beginning to run short, with chronic blight and unemployment in our cities, strong measures will be needed in the years to come. More central economic planning seems inevitable; so do some rather imposing dislocations within our society.

Our system of government, as I said earlier, is based on an imperative of procedural fairness and a concept of limited governmental powers. Others are organized to serve economic imperatives, or imperatives of stability. The most pressing problems of the world and of this country for the foreseeable future are, broadly speaking, economic in nature, and effective solutions to these problems will create dislocations which may well threaten our political stability.

But I believe that this is all the more reason to retain a system whose fundamental object is to maximize individual liberty and whose major premise is that all persons have the right to be heard in matters which affect their interests.

We shall need our checks and balances, our due process of law, our First Amendment, if we are to make the difficult economic choices rationally, fairly, with dignity, and with due regard for the interests of all. If we can no longer say, "That government governs best which governs least," we can still with confidence say, "As government is forced to govern more, that government is still best which impinges least upon the liberty and privacy of the individual," and we have little doubt that the necessary incursions upon private decision-making should reflect and be shaped by a broad-based and informed consensus of the people.

And I believe that our system's guarantees of responsiveness and accountability offer the best hope for a fair and equitable distribution of both the benefits and the burdens of a modern economy. We must summon the courage to demand austerity of ourselves. We must insist upon higher standards of performance from our public officials. We must turn our energies toward solutions to our problems which are future-oriented, not crisis-oriented.

I return to my point of departure, the central role of the impeachment power, as one principal guarantee of accountability, in a government of limited authority. When we have surrendered the power to call our leaders, our decision-makers, to account for the decisions they make in our name, we will have lost the essential quality of political freedom. Given the magnitude of the choices to be made in the future and the consequences for all mankind which depend upon those choices, that quality of freedom is all the more precious.

There is another more immediate and personal lesson to be gleaned from our recent impeachment experience. For all our faults, our materialism, our surface cynicism, our people are brave and decent and steady in a crisis. We have shown that we are capable as a nation of debating and deciding in public with high seriousness and dignity issues of the greatest magnitude.

We should have, and from my travels in recent months I believe we have indeed, derived from the events of the last year and a half a renewed confidence in ourselves and in the adaptability of our system of government to the demands and constraints of the modern world. We can face the challenges of today and tomorrow curiously refreshed by the way in which we have awakened from what President Ford called "our long national nightmare." Now we must face reality with the strength we know we possess. If we do that, the compact with the people can survive intact for the generations to come.

Questions and Discussion

Congressman Rodino's listeners were eager for specifics about the work of the House Judiciary Committee toward the impeachment of President Nixon, and the very first question put to him by the moderator at New England Life Hall,[1] sped to the heart of that matter:

"One of the big uncertainties was the precise meaning of 'high crimes and misdemeanors.' Did you and the committee have a clear concept in mind?"

"Yes, I believe we did, finally, and so did Congress as a whole. Every member of both houses was provided with a copy of a carefully researched document on the origin and history of the concept of impeachment, and while each member had to arrive at a definition of 'high crimes and misdemeanors' for himself, it would have been hard to conclude that the phrase referred to any ordinary violation of a criminal statute, or even any serious violation. What I believe the phrase finally came to mean to Congress was a serious abuse of power. That is, to impeach we had to find that the President had failed to execute the laws of the land carefully and faithfully, to the prejudice of the people and of the Republic And while there was no single specific definition held commonly by every member, all felt that the question at issue was great prejudice to the survival of the Republic, and that the President by his acts had certainly prejudiced its survival."

Other aspects of impeachment were explored at the Parkman House Seminar [2] that evening. It was asked whether dis-

1. Abram T. Collier of New England Life, who presided at the afternoon session in New England Life Hall.
2. In addition to Congressman Peter Rodino and Mrs. Rodino, those present at the Parkman House on the evening of June 16, 1975, were Kevin H. White, Mayor of Boston; Abram T. Collier, Chairman of the Board, New England Mutual Life Insurance Company; Paul Hellmuth, attorney and member of the firm of Hale and Dorr; Arnold Hiatt, President of the Stride Rite Shoe Company of Boston; George V. Higgins, attorney and novelist; Richard Hill,

agreement with his policies or loss of confidence in a President could be sufficient cause. Mr. Rodino thought not, and cited Alexander Hamilton's warning against following a public whim. He felt and others agreed that impeachment over mere disagreement with a President's policies could lead to chaos, as when the Reconstruction Party was determined to remove Andrew Johnson no matter what. It was by a narrow margin that a great miscarriage of intent was averted at that time. Today the majority party in Congress has enough votes to impeach President Ford, but to do so because they disagree with his policies would undermine the system. Impeachment is appropriate only when a man fails to execute the laws he swore to uphold or abuses his powers in a way to subvert the whole constitutional process.

Another significant comment about the nature of impeachment was made by former congressman Jerome Waldie, one of the radio panelists, a former member of the House Judiciary Committee, and a strong accuser of President Nixon.[3] He felt that last year's proceedings established that the people and the House of Representatives will not shrink from using impeachment as a tool of accountability for gross abuse of the Constitution or of presidential powers by any chief executive in future. "If we have done nothing else," he said, "we have

Chairman of the Board, First National Bank of Boston; Pat Jones, Director, Lena Park Community Center, Mattapan; Katherine Kane, Director, Boston 200; Thomas P. O'Neill III, Lieutenant Governor of Massachusetts; Paul Quirk, President, Local 509, Service Employees International Union (AFL-CIO); David L. Rosenbloom, Executive Assistant to the Mayor of Boston; Albert Sacks, Dean of the Harvard Law School; Sam Bass Warner, Jr., Professor of History and Social Science, Boston University.

3. Like other addresses delivered on the Bicentennial Forums, "The Compact with the People" was broadcast on National Public Radio (Sunday, June 22, 1975) and was followed by a question and answer period. Again the moderator was Sander Vanocur in Washington, D.C., and the panelists were George V. Higgins in Boston, attorney and novelist who had also been present at the Parkman House Seminar, and Jerome Waldie, former Democratic member of the House from California, speaking from Philadelphia.

created a restraint on the conduct of Presidents hereafter."

A second question of general interest was how it all came about. Mr. Rodino was asked whether he agreed with Jimmy Breslin, in *How the Good Guys Finally Won,* that it was Rodino and Thomas "Tip" O'Neill of Massachusetts, majority leader of the House, who were able to convince Mr. Nixon to resign. Rodino modestly answered that he thought another book, Theodore White's *The Breach of Faith,* had a better answer: that Mr. Nixon did himself out of office, because he failed to understand the nature of the public trust, because he abused the power that had been given him, and so there came a time when the American people, despite the deception, despite the cover-up, *knew* — and would no longer put up with what they had found out. Mr. Nixon was forced to resign because of the compelling nature of the circumstances that had been revealed. "I don't think it was Mr. O'Neill, I don't think it was me. It was the American people who gave us the right to act, and the constitutional process which removed Mr. Nixon."

The contrasting roles played by the Ervin investigating committee in the Senate and the Judiciary Committee in the House came in for some frank discussion. At one point the televised sessions of the latter were described as "congressional theater," but attorney-novelist George V. Higgins promptly took exception to this statement. The proceedings of this committee were not "theater," he said. "The Ervin committee was theatre and for that reason failed." They were poor investigators but good showmen — indeed, "the grandest Chautauqua" on the subject of presidential accountability that the country has ever seen. Every member of the House Judiciary Committee was up for reelection, so when they spoke frankly they took their political futures in their hands. The same was not true for the members of the Ervin committee. And yet it must be said for the latter that they educated the public about what had been going on, and it is quite possible that the

House Committee could not have accomplished what it did without this preparation. The Ervin committee was very poor in amassing and marshaling evidence. The Rodino committee did that brilliantly, with the help of Mr. Jenner and their counsel, Mr. Doar.

It was also asked what Mr. Rodino thought of the doctrine of Executive Privilege, and he replied that when it comes to the process of impeachment, there are no legal restraints on the ability of the House to make inquiries, regardless of a President's claims to the contrary. Executive privilege is not a statutory right, but a policy which has taken shape by the assertions of a series of recent Presidents in order to maintain separation and privacy from the Congress.

At one point Mr. Waldie was asked why the Republicans in Congress had been so slow to doubt Mr. Nixon, and he answered by drawing an analogy with his own political experience. He reminded the radio audience that Representative Charles Wiggins of California, a close friend, had been one of Mr. Nixon's staunchest defenders on the Judiciary Committee and had probably been shaken more than anyone else in Congress by Mr. Nixon's deceptions. "My only real political hero had been Adlai Stevenson, and I tried to imagine how I would have reacted if someone had told me that Stevenson had committed a crime, and Stevenson had told me that he had not. Now Wiggins and many other Republicans had the same faith in Nixon that I had in Stevenson, and were probably as blind to Nixon's weaknesses as I would have been to Stevenson's. The shattering of their faith was part of the horrible loss that Richard Nixon cost this country."

At New England Life Hall a series of questions on the Nixon pardon were handed up from the floor. Did it not in effect place him above the law? Mr. Rodino answered that he did not challenge President Ford's legal right to grant the pardon, but he did question its coming so soon, and without the hearing of further evidence. Had the system of criminal justice been allowed to proceed as President Ford in his first news conference said it would, the public would probably have accepted whatever he might have done at a later date.

One thoughtful listener in the radio audience felt it was a pity that the full contents of the tapes had never been made public and asked Mr. Waldie what his reaction had been when he heard them.

Waldie replied, "The first time we heard the tapes, I must say, it was a disturbing experience. We were all seated in the Judiciary Committee room with our headphones on, and there was no announcement such as you usually get that 'the next voice you hear will be that of the President of the United States.' Suddenly the system was turned on, you heard a cup and saucer clink, and some embarrassing chatter from a voice you had heard dealing only with momentous issues. My first reaction was embarrassment, partly at what I was hearing, and partly because I felt like an eavesdropper on a conversation too petty to be public. The longer I listened the more I became persuaded that Richard Nixon had no control of the decision-making process. Surprisingly, the most effective voice was John Ehrlichman's. When he and Haldeman and Nixon were talking, Ehrlichman was the only one who did not know that their conversations were being taped. In most of the conversations, Nixon was little more than a bystander, and not a very articulate one at that. When he did make a remark, it frequently had little to do with the subject, and he spent a great deal of time basking in the glories of his *Six Crises*. He came across as simply not up to the responsibility of the White House. That may be an unfair assessment of the whole man, but it is probably a correct assessment of him at that time, in terms of whether we should have gone ahead with the impeachment process. After the pardon I went along with the decision not to do so. I now think that was a mistake. We should at

least have taken a vote in the House. For within three weeks
the House did a remarkable thing. It granted Richard Nixon a
pension of $5000 a month for the rest of his life. This was not
an earned pension, but one that had to be granted by Congress. That vote has muddied the historical record irrevoca-
bly. It put the House on record as having approved his services as President."

At one point it was asked whether the tapes revealed the
President and his aides as competent conspirators. Mr.
Higgins responded that the Godfather would have laughed
himself into convulsions at the way they behaved. They were
rank amateurs. The only one who seemed to get it right was
Haldeman, and he said the reason they kept getting into trouble was that they didn't know how to do these things and
every time they tried they messed it up again. He was quite
right.

One member of the radio audience wanted to know whether
all the President's papers and tapes had been screened by
some member or committee of Congress to discover and clean
up any further possible violations of the public trust, to check
violations and the general integrity of government agencies involved, and any abuses of individual citizens. Mr. Waldie answered that they had not been and certainly should be
thoroughly checked for these purposes. He added that he
thought Congress had the power to do this but would have it
only until pending legal questions as to the ownership of the
tapes had been settled. The questioner said he had been
alarmed to learn that some fifty cases of presidential papers
were at an Air Force base on their way back to Mr. Nixon's
custody.

On this whole issue Mr. Higgins took the opposite view.
He felt that any such exhaustive investigation would deter future advisers from expressing their full and frank opinion on
issues of importance. "I am concerned already that the Presi-

dent's aides and advisers will not feel free to propose alternatives, contingency plans, and opinions, however far out, so that the President may have the benefit of all views. I am afraid they will feel that sometime I or some other journalist will get hold of their documents and make them look bad. I am against wholesale rummaging through Mr. Nixon's papers. He is gone now; let him go."

One member of the audience at New England Life Hall said that St. Clair had recently remarked that the pendulum of power had now swung from the executive to the legislative branch. Mr. Rodino said he did not think so, that the President still has full Constitutional powers, and that President Ford has recently exercised the veto power on a good deal of legislation, including some relating to job opportunities which Congress thought extremely important.

"But behind recent events, we must remember how the system was designed to work. It was intended that Congress should legislate and the Executive should carry out its laws, that the two branches should work in concert, not in opposition, and that neither should be stronger than the other." Congress is composed of 435 people and cannot lead in the sense that the Executive can. But it can and should implement the kind of legislation that is needed.

Mr. Waldie felt that Congress possesses a power of oversight which it has never properly exercised, and that if it had done so, quite possibly it would not have been necessary to impeach President Nixon. With any strong-willed President, there will be friction, and to keep the proper balance Congress must assert its will. One of our great problems is that it has never done so.

We have been talking here about Watergate, Mr. Rodino continued, as if that were our only problem. But there were much deeper abuses of presidential power, particularly in connection with the Vietnam war. "That was a presidential war, one which I think no president could have got Congress to vote for, but which every President since Eisenhower seems to have somehow got Congress quietly to allow. Just how is the critical question to me. I think the President should not have such power unless he can gain the agreement of Congress. To me it is critical that Congress insist that before a President can take such action he must have congressional support."

A Boston banker disagreed with Mr. Rodino on this point and felt that Congress very well represented public opinion during the whole Vietnam affair. "We began with a tiny episode under Eisenhower, a bigger one under Kennedy, and a much bigger one under Johnson. I think that polls of public opinion in those times would have shown general support of these actions up to the last several years of the war. I think Congress represented the mood of its constituents quite closely, even at the time the public mood changed."

One great weakness in our government, Mr. Rodino felt, is the tendency of both Congress and the Executive to revert to politics as usual once a crisis is past. During the deliberations of the Judiciary Committee we saw men and women of different ideologies, different loyalties, black and white, from different parts of the country, coming together and in the main putting aside partisanship and self-interest. They genuinely rose to the occasion, and the public felt this and responded. The result was the cleansing process which was so badly needed, and which restored faith in the system.

"But today the people are once more in a mood of disappointment and frustration, I think because they once more see politicians behaving as politicians, not responding to what the people need but jockeying to win another election. We do have an energy shortage and we do have an economic crisis, and neither is going to be solved by the President and Congress developing their own plans of action at the expense of the other but by the two working together."

Asked what final lesson he would like to leave with his listeners as a result of last year's experience Mr. Rodino said that one thing that impressed him about the American people was that in spite of the expressed fears that they could not stand to go through the impeachment process, that the country would be torn by bitterness and strife, quite the opposite had happened. "The people showed a tremendous capacity to accept and understand a judgment made by their representatives provided that it was decent and fair, and made in such a manner that they could say, 'Our representatives are doing what we expect them to do: they are representing the public interest.' Throughout the country, wherever I have gone, people have seen each other demonstrate a restored faith in the process and the system. I think it is most important that the American people can withstand a crisis, so long as they know that those who govern them can be trusted to hold the reins of government, that they can be believed, that they are fair, that they live up to the letter of the law and the Constitution. As long as we recognize that real security lies in the integrity of our institutions and the informed confidence of the people, our great experiment will survive."

6

The Great American Drift

JOHN V. LINDSAY

It was fitting that this series of Bicentennial Forums should be concluded by John V. Lindsay, two-term mayor of the City of New York. For on Tuesday, July 8, 1975, when he delivered his address, the City of Boston faced many of the problems he had faced. It was still deep in the struggle for integration of its public schools. High unemployment rates, especially among the young, were eating away at neighborhoods. The governor of Massachusetts was slashing programs for human services in the face of a fiscal crisis. New York City was on the verge of bankruptcy. And the federal government continued its policy of domestic retrenchment and the withdrawal of aid to cities.

Mr. Lindsay brought to the occasion the experience of twenty years in government service. A lawyer, he had worked as Executive Assistant to the Attorney General of the United States during the Eisenhower administration. He then served four terms in the House of Representatives, where he specialized in social legislation: civil rights, housing and urban renewal, care of the elderly, aid to education and the arts. A man of energy, imagination, and style, he was elected Mayor of New York City on a wave of hope in 1965 and served in that office until 1973. His mayoralty coin-

cided with the clash between rising popular expectations for urban life and the accumulation of problems unattended since World War II. As Boston's mayor, Kevin White, put it in introducing Mr. Lindsay, he was "the first in America to teach us that there are two sides to a city, the physical and the psychological." He was a national leader who helped bring the needs of cities to public consciousness. He was also the author of the federal revenue-sharing program, the only innovation for direct urban relief that recent Presidents have been willing to support.

"I UNDERSTAND you are preparing to celebrate the 'Fourth.' What for? The doings of that day had no reference to the present . . ."

Those are the words of Abraham Lincoln delivered at Springfield, Illinois, on June 26, 1857. He understood a changing America and changing needs.

And as Abraham Lincoln did, I think we have to ask "What for?" We need to ask that question not because we want to be negative, but because we must understand that flags in our lapels, or parades, or fireworks are no substitute for the real patriotism that has to do with defining the values we want to stand for as a people, and then doing all we can to be true to those values.

The other day I was out at Ellis Island filming a television program on the history of immigration in the United States. And of course I could not take my eyes off the Statue of Liberty looming above the abandoned buildings on the island. It was and has always been to me a constant reminder that the United States, and I might add, the city in which the statue resides, has for most of its history to most of the world stood for freedom and justice. But it is difficult to make that argument today.

I have just spent the better part of a year abroad on a sabbatical, looking at the United States through more distant lenses. The picture, I must say, was not a happy one.

Despite the praise we love to give ourselves every Fourth of July we seem to have given people abroad a different picture. This is because we have too often been willing to compromise our principles abroad under the pretext that foreign affairs must be conducted according to some special set of rules that adhere mainly to manipulation and expediency, not principle and morality.

We have cherished a mythology of American goodness and righteousness while we wantonly destroyed the countryside of Cambodia and Vietnam. Do we really think the world didn't notice the difference between what we were saying and what we were doing?

And, we *still* cherish the notion that individual rights and due process are sacred while we support the alienation of those rights abroad by our support of militaristic and junta governments. And, we *still* cling to the image we have set for ourselves as the "good guys" confronting the evil enemy, when in fact our own CIA has been engaged in the same kind of invidious intrigue abroad that we had always accused the enemy of.

Nothing could be more un-American. Nothing could be calculated to more completely desecrate the memory of those who wrote the Declaration of Independence and those who died for it. And do we really think the world hasn't noticed?

We should be exporting the dream of the colonists — man's time-honored quest for freedom and opportunity. It is time once again for America to be known around the world at least as much for the writings of Jefferson and Lincoln as for the activities of IT&T and Exxon, and the CIA.

We live in a world of extraordinary change and excitement. What seemed impossible a year or two ago suddenly happens

today. The social and political changes taking place worldwide are dramatic and profound: the battle for self-determination and racial equality in Asia and Africa; the economic
struggle of the underdeveloped nations; the new consciousness of women around the world.

Yet America is no longer in the forefront of these movements. Instead we are cautious and silent, resistant of change,
and even aligned with the forces of repression.

On our two-hundredth birthday we have awesome power,
but we also have some characteristics of middle age, especially
an obsession for stability and the status quo. We seem threatened by change rather than excited by it. We too often interpret change in foreign nations not by whether the result is
more democracy for their people but by whether it threatens
the deals we have made, which in any event are increasingly
less trusted. We too often identify America's interest with stability in foreign nations, regardless of the shortcomings or
transgressions of the government in power.

As a result we have shown an embarrassingly high tolerance
for standing with the kinds of oppressive and corrupt regimes
we defied 199 years ago. It is hard to imagine Thomas Jefferson standing arm in arm with Papa Doc, or General Thieu, or
General Park, or the Greek junta, or Franco. But now on the
eve of our Bicentennial we seem to accept these kinds of alliances on the pretext that they are essential to our national security and that no matter how bad these regimes may be the
alternatives would be worse. And so we have closed our eyes
to torture, murder, repression, and thievery — and in the process we have turned our Statue of Liberty into a relic of the
past instead of a living symbol of what we stand for around
the world.

I believe we can be better than that.

I believe we can use this Bicentennial period to reexamine a cynical, manipulative foreign policy that sees the nations of the world as so many pieces on a chessboard and ignores the people who live there.

We must make our Bicentennial something more than a bonanza for fireworks-makers and parade-watchers. We must use it as a time to look at ourselves candidly and rededicate ourselves to our proud heritage in a way that once again makes the word America synonymous in all languages for hope and freedom. The first standard of our foreign policy should be that it is concerned with exporting justice and self-determination and freedom. That is the standard our heritage demands. That is the way we can win *real* allies among the people of the developed and the developing nations abroad. And, in fact, that is the standard that is most consistent with an honest definition of "national security" — for national security in the end means very little if the nation we secure is one that stands for little and has lost the confidence of hundreds of millions of the world's peoples.

And just as we will be judged by what we do abroad, we will also be watched for the principles we follow at home.

Here again as we celebrate this Fourth of July, we must ask "What for?" because, in Lincoln's words, "The doings of that day had no reference to the present." What does America stand for to the child growing up hungry in the South Bronx or in Appalachia? How do we explain our celebration to women denied jobs or to the elderly and poor who are denied food in a country that spends billions a year to feed pets?

And what is most disturbing to me about the plight of these whom the American dream has left behind is that on the eve of the Bicentennial there seems to be growing sentiment throughout the country that government must now turn its back on them. Under a battle cry of no more big government, or no more profligate social programs, a curious unwitting coalition seems to have developed of three separate groups.

First, reformed liberals — leaders of the great society who now give every appearance of running for cover. Second, conservatives — who always preached against big government and are now surprised to find some old opponents stealing their issue. And third, newly elected officials who say they are speaking candidly, speak of not raising false expectations with political promises, of a time at hand for a governmental do-nothing approach to American society. This unlikely coalition is preaching, essentially, a doctrine of no-action government.

I submit that 200 years of American history should make clear that "no-action government" is unacceptable as a guiding principle, for it is, essentially, leaderless government.

It is said by some that government of the sixties overpromised. That government of the sixties raised excessive expectations. That may be legitimately arguable. But I do not believe the response of the seventies should be to revel in leaderlessness: A response of *no* promises, *no* expectations, *no* goals, *no* standards, *no* action, and . . . *no* hope.

If we can justifiably celebrate anything on our Bicentennial it is our strong, irrevocable tradition of government leadership and commitment — morally, legally, and with action programs — to help the less fortunate, to protect the deprived, and to build a better society. I believe we should recommit ourselves to that tradition of American initiative — humane and restrained, yet daring and determined. That I believe is the real challenge. Not *whether* to act, but how and according to what principles, what priorities and what morality.

We tried in the sixties to combat fear and want and illness. Of course, we didn't eliminate these conditions. But that is not to say we failed, that it was all wasted and misguided. We accomplished much. There are thousands of former drug addicts now holding jobs and paying taxes; countless children who received medical attention, decent meals, education, and affection through Head Start; former welfare mothers who have used day care and job training to make themselves productive and tax-paying citizens, and high school dropouts brought back and sent on to college by the pioneering street academies. Those are tangible accomplishments.

More important, but incalculable, we opened up government to a new generation of leaders, educated and trained in the harsh realities of the streets. Through the poverty program and other initiatives, many started by fighting City Hall. They soon learned that it was better to run and win and become part of the action at City Hall. Nothing could be *more* American. It has brought stability and excitement to our politics. And it was a worthwhile investment of tax revenues.

At the same time, we should have learned from our mistakes. Just as these problems won't go away by ignoring them, they won't be solved in five to ten years. We should learn from Model Cities and Manpower Training and Head Start how to do it better. Yes, we should be skeptical, and careful. But America should be mature enough to learn and grow and move forward.

After all, those critics in Washington never showed such impatience with the staggering cost overruns of the C–5A. That was for defense. And they failed to show such concern for efficiency and performance with Lockheed when it was bailed out of bankruptcy. That was private enterprise. And they seemed unperturbed when the Environmental Protection Act fell far short of its 1975 goals. That, we were told, just needed some more realistic redefinition.

But the cities, the poor, the blacks are held to a different standard. Their programs are the programs of profligacy.

Beyond this obvious double standard, we should also realize that much of the talk about failures of government action and the absence of government responsibility is hypocritical. For example, our mayors have been going hat in hand to Washington for a decade seeking help. For years they warned of the fiscal crisis which now threatens our major cities as never before. Occasionally they were thrown a bone or two. Usually they were told that they were profligate, that mayors should be self-reliant and live within their means, that Congress and the White House were not responsible.

But our cities didn't inflict these monumental American problems on themselves. They have borne the impact of strong American *national* policies and priorities — one after another, with devastatingly destructive effect. For *twenty* years, Washington sponsored and underwrote the flight of the middle class to the suburbs with massive subsidies for highways and FHA housing. And *nothing* was given for urban mass transit and urban housing for the middle groups who stayed. For forty years we have watched tens of millions of less fortunate citizens flee from rural and southern areas - - poor whites, blacks, and Spanish — seeking jobs and opportunities in the cities. And the welfare system local governments are forced to fund is not the creation of New York or Boston or Philadelphia, but of Washington. And it has been imposed on local people and the local property tax in the most unworkable form possible. It remains America's greatest scandal — not because of its generosity or fraud, but because of its discrimination and bureaucracy and antiwork ethic — a nonproductive American system that the American federal government refuses to reform, and which only it can do.

So it was *misguided* government action in Washington, America's proud capital, that then brought despair to the American city. But now, in the name of no-action government the American city is being told that help is not available. The absence of funds is not the *real* problem. It is the absence of leadership that is the problem.

And so it is with so many of our other problems. American cities and suburbs suffer from a reign of terror. But they are told that law enforcement is a local matter, while the federal government blindly sanctions the endless flood of guns that pour across state lines and poison the peace of American streets. American consumers suffer from dangerous products, deceptive advertising, and prices that rarely react to competitive pressures. But Americans are told that the answer is an end to government regulation, when in fact that deliberate avoidance of effective regulation has generated many of the problems.

And throughout the country, millions of Americans desperate for work are told that government action to guarantee them a job would be ill advised because the government must retrench — when in fact it was misguided federal economic policies that put them out of work.

Like it or not, government will continue to be a major force in our lives. There are always opportunities to cutback, restructure, or speed the process; every bureaucracy, and certainly our federal regulatory agencies, can use shaking up and pressure to produce better and faster. But the notion that active *initiative government* is the major cause of our collective woes just won't hold up. It is an easy scapegoat because just about everybody can find something to complain about.

The answer is not a retreat from government action. We no longer live in a world where you and I as individuals can match the extraordinary power and scope of corporations and labor unions. Effective governmental action is essential to the protection of individual rights and the guarantee of personal choice. We do not live in the same simple agrarian economy as the colonists, where individual power was preeminent. That was the time when we were the land of plenty, and we built a whole political concept based on plenty. Now we must change. We must realize the limits of our energy, land, and other resources. We need careful government planning to preserve, conserve, and allocate, and to do this properly we shall need government action more than ever.

Those who preach to us today about the glory of individual initiative conveniently ignore the overweening grasp on the marketplace of multinational institutions, run from private executive suites, that hold more power than most foreign governments. Only government action can monitor their conduct and ensure protection for the millions of individuals they deal with.

Only a careful government program could guarantee sound private pension systems and basic worker rights, could safeguard the rights of the farmworkers to organize and be represented by the union of their choice as just accomplished in California, could force safety and health standards on reluctant industries ranging from drugs to cars to cigarettes, or could prohibit the red-lining of urban houses by banks and insurance companies, thereby contributing to the deterioration of whole neighborhoods.

These are instances where thousands, even millions, of unorganized Americans suffer from the dominating effect of private economic power. These are cases where the preservation of individual freedom and economic security demands government action.

Americans quite readily accept the appeal of no-action government when they think about welfare costs and bungling bureaucrats, but they won't tolerate government inaction when it comes to *their* pension, *their* job rights, or *their* home mortgages.

The notion has spread today that someone else is always getting a better deal. The working man attacks government programs for the poor but demands greater unemployment insurance and pension protection. The agricultural states criticize urban programs as discriminatory, despite years of farm price supports and rural economic development. We have seen an erosion of America's commitment to aid the less fortunate. Nothing is more disturbing in this Bicentennial period than this new divisiveness that pits one deprived group against another so that each blames the other for government's failure to meet their needs. This has bred a peculiarly American form of social polarization. Breeding fear as it goes, it has been the feeding ground for a new breed of American political demagogues who have risen to power by playing on those fears, never searching out their real causes.

Instead, we must all realize that in every corner of the nation there remain today important challenges for government action. And to solve some of the worst deteriorations of the quality of life in America, *there can be no substitute* for new priorities, and even new money.

This does not automatically mean more taxes. In the first place, local governments and local people are overtaxed as it is. They can take no more. It does mean federal reorganization of the tax structure to make it equitable from place to place and from class to class. And it also means choosing those things that are most important for our future.

But money is not the most important part of government action, and we cannot allow self-styled conservatives to suggest that the debate is between liberal spenders who waste money and conservatives who understand the limits and value of money. *That* is *not* the debate. Program-oriented people understand the limits of money only too well, and certainly better than those who support bottomless military budgets and cost overruns. They have to. They're watched and monitored far more closely. No, the real debate is over the vigorous exercise of government's *moral* and *legal* powers. The men who were once called the "great spenders" for human needs — the authors of the New Deal and the Great Society — are not remembered today for the money they spent as much as for their vision of a better America and their commitment to the struggle for individual rights and liberties. And today our response should be based on the magnitude and intensity of the human needs we see all around us. In the past these responses, imperfect as they were, were not cold calculated financial transactions, but the exercise of a compassionate, concerned, humane government.

By contrast, spokesmen for government nonaction in recent years have in reality opposed not only government spending but government leadership as well. And we should judge them in the same way — not by the dollars they claim to save, but by the value they place on the lives and health and property of our people. We have heard them preach about protection of individual liberties, but they have been willing to ignore blatant discrimination in voting against blacks and against women in employment.

They talk about individual initiative but watch children go deprived of the education and training necessary to compete effectively in this modern economy. They worship the principle of free enterprise, yet they accept those massive conglomerates that dominate the marketplace and even the federal agencies supposedly created to monitor and control their actions. Perhaps most surprising, these self-proclaimed conservatives were strangely silent when the White House tapped newsmen's phones, when the FBI conducted illegal infiltration of peaceful organizations, when the CIA opened personal mail, and when the President invented a sweeping doctrine of executive privilege that rewrote the constitutional balance of powers. As I understand the tradition of conservative thought, it clearly and forcefully condemns each of these practices, but instead we have learned that the new American conservatism believes in individual liberties except where they might conflict with some vague concept of "national security."

It is as if they had added those words as qualifying language to the Bill of Rights. Wouldn't this have amazed Jefferson, Adams, Madison, and Franklin, those supreme patriots, who fought against oppressive government power that indiscriminately violated the sanctity of individual rights. *Their* legacy was never meant to be a doctrine of national security to justify overweening, unchecked national power.

That is not the message of Lexington and Concord. Of course, we must be strong. And God knows we are strong. America will not fall for lack of strength, or bombs or guns. Indeed, the doctrine of national security developed in recent times has brought us to the edge of tyranny, not freedom.

It masterminded the Vietnam war, and finally, through Watergate, it corrupted American government. And even now, it so dominates our national consciousness that in the aftermath of Vietnam, instead of learning the limits of power and destruction we are again galloping down the same old road. Another $725 million for the B–1 bomber; $203 million more for fifty Minutemen II Intercontinental Ballistic Missiles; $690 million for the purchase of more AWACS planes. The challenge is not just to blindly arm again, but to discipline ourselves to some priorities and to learn how to *use* our strength, both abroad and at home.

We must seize the opportunity of the Bicentennial to look at ourselves on these terms and to redirect ourselves. On our next birthday, what kind of country do we want to be? Do we want to be an America that uses its strength to fight blindly for a merchant ship, without waiting for either facts or negotiation because we decide that firm decisive action will have important symbolic value, while at the same time in the name of no-action government we ignore equally significant symbolism and harsher reality by *refusing* to use our strength to save our American cities at home?

I believe we can be better than that. America can once again be a source of hope for the world. We can once again be the land of opportunity for the poor. America can once again be a society that genuinely seeks peace, instead of glorying in violence. America can be the kind of society where the rule of law, not the gun, is the great equalizer.

Yes, we must have a healthy skepticism of government action. But we cannot be pressured into letting this become simple and cold negativism.

We must remember that the government that refuses to make *any* promises is a government that provides no leadership, and indeed sets no goals for its poeple. Those who preach no-action government may well be using it to hide their timidity and moral neutrality — and to avoid the harsher and very real problems of our time because of the political dangers they contain. Now, more than ever, we need government action to provide jobs, education, and food to the poor. America needs to fulfill the promise of equal opportunity for minorities and women, to bring mass transportation systems, safe streets, and fiscal stability to its cities. The Bicentennial is no time to turn our backs, to pretend that America is something different than it is, or that it now after these last years stands for something meaningful and lasting abroad, which it does not.

Finally, governmental action is essential because it is the expression of our collective will. It is the way our society expresses its commitment to equal opportunity, to adequate health care, schooling, and housing, and to an improvement of our standard of living.

We *each* have a dream for ourselves and for our families, but we must also have a collective dream for America, not just an idyllic picture of millions of affluent individuals doing their own thing free of government leadership. *That* notion ended with the spinning wheel.

Instead, we must have dreams like Thomas Jefferson's. Dreams like Abe Lincoln's. Dreams like Martin Luther King's. Dreams for a better society. In fact, maybe the best thing we

Americans can do on our Bicentennial is dream of what we want to be able to celebrate five or ten years from now, and dedicate ourselves to fulfilling those dreams. Maybe then, we will celebrate an America that truly stands for freedom and justice and hope at home and abroad.

Maybe, then, we will celebrate an America where Watts as well as Westchester, and Brownsville as well as Brookline, are places we can be proud of.

Maybe then we will celebrate an America where handguns are kept out of civilian hands because we hate violence and death more than we love symbols of manhood.

Maybe then we will celebrate an America where dissent and diversity are once again honored and protected.

Maybe then we will celebrate an America where anyone who wants to work can get a job, and anyone who is sick can get a doctor.

I dream, and I believe, we can have that kind of celebration. Such dreams are the worthy heritage of 200 years. And together we must carry them forward.

Questions and Discussion

THE PLIGHT OF THE CITIES

Such a broad-ranging speech was bound to call forth diverse reactions. There were questions about the control of corporations, unemployment and economic planning, Europe's present opinion of us, inflation, and recession.

But more than any other topic, Mayor Lindsay's questioners [1] were interested in exploring his experience with

1. Members of the Parkman House Seminar, July 8, 1975, were Kevin H. White, Mayor of Boston; Harold Amos, Professor of Microbiology and Molecu-

urban problems, their causes, and possible remedies. Particularly in the years since World War II, white flight and the influx of poor ethnic minority groups have created a steadily shrinking tax base in the inner cities. At the same time suburbia came to distrust the inner city and to blame it for many of America's problems. Mayor Lindsay strongly felt that federal policies were responsible for a large share of the trouble. Among such policies were the underwriting of extensive highway building and hence easy commuting, ready mortgages from the FHA, and the actual discouragement of railways and public transportation. He also felt that some urban problems, such as joblessness and the steadily growing demand for poor-relief, were by-products of the general national condition and should therefore be a federal responsibility, not solely that of the cities and states, as they have been until now.

Finally, he felt that a decision of the Supreme Court, intended to strengthen the representation of cities in state legislatures against shrinking agricultural populations, had ironically had the unexpected effect of weakening the cities against their new rivals, the suburbs. Mayor Lindsay recalled a private luncheon in honor of retired Supreme Court Chief-Justice

lar Genetics, Harvard Medical School; Louise Bonar, Boston Public Schools, Citywide Coordinating Council; David Broder, reporter, the Washington *Post,* Abram T. Collier, Chairman of the Board, New England Mutual Life Insurance Company; John Finnegan, Representative to the Great and General Court of Massachusetts; Doby Flowers, Deputy Director of Community Development, City of Boston; Barry Gottehrer, Executive Director, Life Insurance Association of Massachusetts; Howard W. Johnson, Chairman of the Corporation, Massachusetts Institute of Technology; Katherine Kane, Director, Boston 200; Dr. and Mrs. S. Charles Kastin; Emily Lloyd, Transportation Advisor to the Mayor of Boston; Gerry Marcinowski, Deputy Director, Office of Public Service, City of Boston; Arthur Naparstek, Director of Policy Planning and Program Development, National Center for Urban Ethnic Affairs, Washington, D.C.; Elaine Noble, Representative to the Great and General Court of Massachusetts; George Rockwell, President, State Street Bank; David L. Rosenbloom, Executive Assistant to the Mayor of Boston; David Smith, Professor of Political Science, University of Massachusetts, College III, Boston; Sam Bass Warner, Jr., Professor of History and Social Science, Boston University; Thomas Winship, editor, the Boston *Globe.*

Earl Warren, at which Warren said the most important decision in his time was *Baker* v. *Carr*, the "one man one vote" ruling, which forced the reapportionment of state legislatures according to population. By this decision all cities lost voice, but to the rising suburbs, not to the rural areas. New York City, for example, lost four or five seats in the legislature to Nassau County, and the result was a radical shift in power and a profound weakening of the city.

FINANCIAL DIFFERENCES

The financial motives that forced people out of the cities continue to affect urban revenues. Mayor Lindsay recalled that one bad fight he went through was to secure a contributing tax from commuters who worked in the city. Most political scientists agree that the best ratio for any such regional tax is for commuters to pay one half of what residents pay. But the best ratio New York could secure was one eighth, with the result that there is still a strong incentive to live in the suburbs.

Asked how urban and suburban America can ultimately be brought back together, Mayor Lindsay replied that one cynical answer is that it can't happen until enough misery besets the suburbs. In New York some suburbs are beginning to suffer urban discomforts. For example, welfare last year took 60 percent of the budget in Westchester County, a wealthy residential area just outside the city. The increase in the crime rate is higher in the suburban counties of Westhester, Nassau, and Suffolk than in New York City. When enough things of this kind occur, when the misery level gets high enough, something will happen. For example, basic welfare reform came within an inch of passing two Congresses ago, because of suburban pressure to get the welfare burden off the property tax. "Quite realistically," Mayor Lindsay said, "I think the cities and the suburbs will someday find that their problems even out, and when that happens the differences in their interests and outlooks will disappear."

TAXATION

Many national as well as urban problems stem from the lack of a uniform tax structure throughout the country. "Few nations in the world," Mr. Lindsay said, "and none in Europe that I know of, have a patchwork system of taxation like ours, which varies from city to city and state to state." Most nations structure their national and local tax systems together so that they have a unified system and a uniformly motivated population, not a disunited country where businessmen and corporations seek tax havens.

"When I was in Congress the Ways and Means Committee decided it ought to figure out what was really wrong with the tax structure of the United States by examining local taxes as they dovetailed with federal taxes. It assigned the task to a special committee of the Judiciary Committee, of which I was a member. A very competent professional staff spent several years in hearings and research. They did their job well. By the time the reports emerged I was mayor of New York, and the volumes of documentation would have made a pile that reached the top of this stage. But nothing was done with them. Absolutely nothing!"

In the United States we have reached a point where the multiplication of taxes is such that a federal overhaul of most state and local arrangements is the only way to create a more equitable system throughout the nation and to stop the flight of people from place to place for tax reasons. George McGovern tried to tackle this issue and was roundly thrashed — in part for his efforts on the problem. When you take up tax issues you run into more sacred cows than anyone could imagine. As things now stand it would be a courageous politician indeed who would take on the subject of basic tax reform.

STRIKES

Asked about the power of government employees' unions, Mayor Lindsay felt that it had been too great and cited his experience in several well-known confrontations. The famous garbage strike, he said, was not wanted by the union leadership but was brought about by a group of insurgents who refused to accept an arbitration agreement which had been accepted by the management of the disposal companies, the city, and the union. As a result the city became a monumental shambles which took weeks to clean up.

What ultimately checked the growing power of the unions was counterpressure brought to bear by the general public. In a wildcat police strike, the president of the union, "an enormously decent man," was so sick and unhappy he said that in about six months he would resign from the union and he did. The militants were convinced that they had only to push the same old button and the mayor would cave in. But at last the people turned against them. One councilman, whose neighbors included many policemen, said the people were yelling at the cops and calling them names. When the people didn't back the cops, the strike petered out.

But the worst of all was the teachers' strike, which was about power, not money. The Board of Education and the Teachers' Union had merged into one solid glacial mass which nothing could budge. You couldn't move an eraser or a piece of paper, much less affect the quality of public school education. The hardest thing for established groups to do is give up power, and that is what this strike was all about. We were trying to take power from the Board of Education and give it to the neighborhoods, including the power of the budget. But the Board and the president of the Teachers' Union, Albert Shanker, both refused to give up power, and the strike went on much too long. Even in the first budgetary meetings when we were planning for this decentralization, the Board of Education refused a million dollars for the training of budgetary experts in the neighborhoods so that local boards could learn to function and be accountable. We then had another fight to reorganize the Board to make it decentralization-minded, and that started my troubles with Shanker, who foresaw a fight for control.

THE CITY UNIVERSITY

But not all crises in the city's educational systems grew out of strikes, though power was never far from the central issue. Whenever you deal with a polarized situation you make choices based on that fact. And it is never easy. "You never can choose between good and bad; you have only a choice between evils. Yet I still believe we did the right thing when we sensed the beginning of a blow-up between black and white over the University of the City of New York." There was a student body of some 200,000, about half full-time and half part-time, with an impending collision between whites and nonwhites which was going to make the clash with Shanker look easy. The black community began charging that the whites (largely Jewish) were keeping the blacks out, and the whites were saying that the various efforts to bring blacks in were displacing their more qualified sons and daughters. Things were fast moving toward a head-on, no-win collision. So one day we announced open enrollment — any high school graduate would be admitted to the university — and the polarization ended overnight!

Of course this policy also created havoc overnight. Freshman enrollment jumped 25 percent the first year, professors resigned because they felt the quality of education would be destroyed, so we had to raise their salaries enough to make it impossible for them to resign. But after two years others flocked to New York, intellectuals electrified by the experiment. The majority of students remained white, and over half these were Catholic — which told us something about the blue-collar class. We learned that the City University was an important anchor for the working man, because as soon as he moved to the suburbs he lost free higher education for his children. But most importantly, perhaps, we averted a serious racial collision.

ABSORBING THE IMMIGRANTS

Not surprisingly, New York's solution to its educational problems was not unrelated to its handling of immigrant groups. Ethnically New York is the most mixed city in the world, and the city has always absorbed into its class, occupational, and neighborhood structure all the groups that came. The Irish became police, the Italians sanitation workers, the Jewish groups, largely from eastern Europe, teachers. All these were rapidly absorbed into the middle class, won great power in the process, and spilled over into the suburbs.

Western Europe is beginning to experience this process but is looking to a different solution. There the Mediterraneans and Turks and Africans become street sweepers and workers of the lowest class. Here there is steady movement upward: our city hospital staffs are a heartening example. It is unthinkable for the middle class in Europe to move over and make room for a new bourgeoisie. The problem is always acute when the newest group is of another color, and that is true here as well as in Europe.

A part of New York's ability to absorb immigrant groups comes from the fact that government is often the employer of both the first and the last resort. And I am convinced that an equally important element is decentralization. There is less of a busing problem in New York today than there is in some other cities because the many ethnic and racial neighborhoods which have control over their own schools are all convinced that they are getting education of equal quality. Secure in this belief, they feel no need for change.

DECENTRALIZATION AND THE NEIGHBORHOOD

Not only in school affairs but in many other ways New York is a city of neighborhoods, and the neighborhood is the building block of the city. Families can't stay together if the neighborhoods don't have the support systems they need. If the public actions aren't right at the neighborhood level, whether it be code enforcement, zoning, education, or taxation, then come inequity and insecurity, a lack of options, alienation, and anger. Yet there is no national policy for maintaining the viability of neighborhoods.

Mayor Lindsay was asked whether he saw any possibility of developing a neighborhood policy on the national level, perhaps one modeled on the current environmental impact statement. He thought such a policy could be devised, but that three ingredients would be essential: uniform national standards, parity among neighborhoods, and local responsibility and accountability. Because our public housing policies do not include these three requirements but insist on "scattering" (the opposite of neighborlike grouping of tenants), the building of new public housing in New York has come to a standstill.

Some interesting comments on the place of neighborhood action in city government were made by the members of the radio audience and panelists Stanley L. Newman of New York and Mayor Lawrence D. Cohen of St. Paul, Minnesota.[2] Mr. Newman said that in New York there were many local councils and "no lack of a sense of community" but that their effect depended on cooperation by the mayor and the city government. Mayor Cohen agreed and mentioned that St. Paul was about to establish seventeen community councils, a citizens' "early warning system." He said that in nearly every area of government the citizen wants to know what is happening and to have a voice in decisions which will affect his neighborhood.

AMERICAN TYPES AND STEREOTYPES

The radio audience also reflected views far to the right and far to the left of the mainstream, types and stereotypes which Mayor Lindsay had almost prophetically mentioned. There was the woman schoolteacher from a small city in Middle America who lamented our lack of moral values. She had recently been to a teachers' convention where she had examined the textbooks on display and found in them "plenty of excitement, but not one thread of moral value." There was the big-city lawyer who felt that government per se is evil and

2. Mayor Lindsay's address was broadcast over Public Radio Sunday evening, July 13. The moderator was Robert Cromie, a free-lance journalist, and the two gentlemen named above. Mr. Newman had worked at the U.S. Department of Housing and Urban Development and the Model Cities Program. In 1973 Mayor Lindsay appointed him to the New York State Planning Commission, and he is now Vice President of the New York City Planning and Exhibition Corporation. Mayor Cohen was formerly director of the University of Minnesota Law School.

who was fighting sex education, busing, and taxation. And there was the mathematician turned carpenter who felt alienated from most of what is going on in America and said he was impressed by most of what Mayor Lindsay had said but felt powerless to influence events. This speaker drew the sympathy of Mayor Cohen, who cited his own experience in sponsoring social programs which were promptly vetoed while the military budget continued to go up and up. Mr. Newman added that the present indifference among young people was in sharp contrast with the feeling in the sixties, when they were receptive to new ideas, change, and experiment. This whole discussion was highly reminiscent of the views of the lady from Utah who had called in twice on earlier programs to express with real eloquence her sense of helplessness.

A NEW LEADERSHIP

Asked where a new leadership with an understanding of urban problems would come from, Mr. Lindsay expressed confidence that a new younger group of leaders would come forward to maintain the republic. "I think a lot of young people are coming along to rebuild the base of the political system. I think of my own generation and its loss of leaders through war. My college roommate should be President of the United States today — but he was killed on Okinawa. Then I think of the whole generation that has had no political experience except Vietnam and Watergate. Many of this generation are growing vegetables on mountaintops and saying to hell with it. But many are being reaccepted into the broken system. If we can get enough of that generation to turn around and face the system, they will come back. But it has to be a system they can believe in."

133

The system one could believe in seemed, in retrospect, to lie at the root of Mr. Lindsay's thinking. The neighborhood, local control, decentralized power, and administration were his proposals for the restoration of public faith. Participation in affairs of immediate concern would both do justice among racial and ethnic groups, and would restore confidence in politics. Here the young people would receive their training for later national roles, and here would arise the necessary new fount of energy and power for an active, responsive government. On our two-hundredth birthday what we needed most was to be born again.